# SPY NOTES

## McINERNEY'S BRIGHT LIGHTS, BIG CITY

### JANOWITZ'S SLAVES OF NEW YORK

### ELLIS'S LESS THAN ZERO

... AND ALL THOSE OTHER HIP URBAN NOVELS OF THE 1980S

*including*

- *Biographical Notes*
- *Plot Summaries and Commentaries*
- *Questions for Review*
- *Suggested Theme Topics*
- *A Simulated Rap Session with the Authors*
- *A Master Genre-in-a-Nutshell Comparison Chart*
- *The Revolutionary NOVEL-O-MATIC™ Fiction-Writing Device*

## by the editors of SPY

**A SPY BOOK**
**DOLPHIN/DOUBLEDAY**
New York   London   Toronto   Sydney   Auckland

**DOUBLEDAY**
is a division of Bantam Doubleday Dell Publishing Group Inc. Cliffs ® Notes is published by Cliffs Notes, Inc. *SPY NOTES* is a parody of Cliffs Notes and is published by Doubleday, a division of Bantam Doubleday Dell Publishing Group Inc. Doubleday is not affiliated with, nor is this parody authorized by Cliffs ® Notes or Cliffs Notes, Inc.

*SPY NOTES* is also a satire of Jay McInerney's *Bright Lights, Big City*, *Ransom* and *Story of My Life*; Tama Janowitz's *American Dad*, *Slaves of New York* and *A Cannibal in Manhattan*; Bret Easton Ellis's *Less Than Zero* and *The Rules of Attraction*; Jill Eisenstadt's *From Rockaway*; Lisa Grunwald's *Summer*; Peter J. Smith's *Highlights of the Off-Season*; Mark Lindquist's *Sad Movies*; Peter Farrelly's *Outside Providence*; Kristen McCloy's *Velocity*; Lisa Pliscou's *Higher Education*; David Foster Wallace's *The Broom of the System*; Nancy Lemann's *Lives of the Saints*; Mary-Ann T. Smith's *The Book of Phoebe*; Susan Minot's *Monkeys*; and Michael Chabon's *The Mysteries of Pittsburgh*.

*Writer* Paul Simms

*Design* Alex Isley Design

*Research* Bob Mack
Elissa Schappell
Eddie Stern
Caren Weiner

*Contributors* Joanne Gruber
Eric Kaplan
Sally Lapiduss

A Dolphin Book
Published by Doubleday, a division of Bantam Doubleday Dell
Publishing Group, Inc.
666 Fifth Avenue, New York, New York 10103
**Dolphin, Doubleday,** and the portrayal of two dolphins are trademarks of Doubleday, a division of Bantam Doubleday Dell Publishing Group, Inc.

LIBRARY OF CONGRESS CATALOGING-IN-PUBLICATION DATA
Spy notes on McInerney's bright lights, big city, Janowitz's slaves of New York, Ellis's
   less than zero, and others / the editors of Spy.—1st ed.
       p.   cm.
   "A Dolphin book"
   ISBN 0-385-24745-1
   1. American fiction—History and criticism—Humor.   2. Criticism—
Humor.   I. Spy (New York, N.Y.)
PS138.S69   1989
813'.54'0207—dc19          89-1255
                        CIP

Copyright © 1989 by SPY PUBLISHING PARTNERS, L.P.
All Rights Reserved
Printed in the United States of America
September 1989
First Edition

# CONTENTS

NOVEL-O-MATIC™ Fiction-Writing Device (detachable)

# INTRODUCTION

In September 1984, Vintage Contemporaries published a novel called *Bright Lights, Big City* by a 29-year-old writer named Jay McInerney. The author's youth and the racy, semi-autobiographical depiction of drug abuse, sexual promiscuity and post-adolescent angst in the mid-1980s almost made *Bright Lights, Big City* a celebrated best-seller.

More important, the novel's success spawned a whole new literary canon—a genre defined by young authors and their equally racy, semi-autobiographical depictions of drug abuse, sexual promiscuity and post-adolescent angst in the mid-1980s. That the books were at best work-manlike, unenlightening and formulaic was overshadowed by the authors' burning desire to write and to be written about.

*Less Than Zero, Slaves of New York, Story of My Life* . . . each new novel was an additional brush stroke that more clearly defined the unwritten manifesto of the genre. Each protagonist, for example, grappled unsuccessfully with moodiness and indecision. Each protagonist ruminated endlessly on the hollowness of his condition and subsequent bad mood. Each protagonist had a mother who died. And so on.

As the era of high-style cocaine abuse and wanton promiscuity faded into the past, so did the reading public's fascination with the novels that chronicled it. Nonetheless, this 1980s genre made an indelible mark in literary history—a mark as prominent and enduring as the Flemish picaresque novel of the early 1800s, the "automatic writing" craze of the 1920s or the American gothic romance novel of the late 1970s. Thus, these novels of the 1980s—individually and as a genre—probably merit serious analysis and discussion of some sort, lest they be completely forgotten in the future.

# BIOGRAPHICAL NOTE

Jay McInerney (MACK-ih-nur-nee) was born in Hartford, Connecticut, in 1955. He attended Williams College, where he met his future editor, Gary Fisketjon. After spending two years in Japan on a fellowship, he worked for seven months as a fact checker at *The New Yorker* before being fired in 1980. He then worked as a reader of unsolicited manuscripts at Random House, his future publisher. During this time, he was married and then divorced.

Fisketjon introduced him to the writer Raymond Carver, who urged McInerney to enroll in his Syracuse University writing program. At Syracuse, McInerney met his second wife, Merry Reymond, a graduate student who at first thought McInerney was "a show-off and a jerk." He tried to write his first novel, *Ransom*, but could not finish it. He then wrote *Bright Lights, Big City* over a six-week period in 1983. He and Merry married in June 1984. *Bright Lights, Big City* was published by Vintage Contemporaries, a new trade paperback series designed to appeal to young urban professionals. After selling the film rights, McInerney wrote three drafts of the script. Finally, he was removed from the project. The film was neither a commercial nor a critical success.

Due to the success of *Bright Lights, Big City*—the book—McInerney returned to his first writing effort. Vintage published *Ransom*, which received uniformly negative reviews. Undaunted, McInerney went to the writers' colony Yaddo, where he wrote *Story of My Life*, noted for its deliberate lack of quotation marks. *Story of My Life* was published by Atlantic Monthly Press, where Fisketjon now worked. Of an initial printing of over 100,000 copies, *Story of My Life* reportedly sold fewer than 20,000 (though McInerney himself estimates it sold between 65,000 and 85,000 copies).

# *Bright Lights, Big City* by Jay McInerney

## LIST OF CHARACTERS

### Jamie Conway

A young man who lives in New York City, works at a magazine much like *The New Yorker* and goes to the nightclubs every night to take cocaine. His mother died of cancer.

### Tad Allagash

Jamie's friend who goes to the nightclubs every night and encourages Jamie to take cocaine.

### Amanda

Jamie's wife, who left him. She is a fashion model.

### Megan Avery

One of Jamie's sympathetic co-workers.

### Michael Conway

Jamie's younger brother. Because Jamie doesn't want to think about his dead mother, he avoids Michael.

## 1. "IT'S SIX A.M. DO YOU KNOW WHERE YOU ARE?"

### Summary

Jamie is at an all-night discothèque with Tad. They have been using cocaine. Jamie talks to a girl with a shaved head. He goes into the bathroom and takes some cocaine. He asks a woman to dance, but she declines. He goes to the ladies' bathroom with a different woman. They take cocaine together and discuss how "all the good words" start with the letters "D" and "L." After this witty banter, the girl decides to leave.

Jamie leaves the nightclub and walks past the apartment he once shared with Amanda, remembering how pleasant their life seemed before they married. Then he sits on a pier overlooking the Hudson River and thinks about all the things that are wrong with his life.

### Historical Note

*Bright Lights, Big City* made quite a splash in the New York literary scene when it was first published, because it was written in the *second-person* narrative voice. Rather than saying "I go to nightclubs" (first-person) or "He goes to nightclubs" (third-person), McInerney wrote "You go to nightclubs." Because the protagonist is never given a name in this format, there was much speculation about what real person the character was based on, although most critics assumed that the book was semi-autobiographical. Like the protagonist, McInerney lived in New York, worked at *The New Yorker*, got fired, tried to be a writer, had many stories rejected by many magazines, took cocaine, went to nightclubs with sophisticated bachelor friends, was divorced and wrote a book about it all.

It was not until McInerney wrote the movie script for *Bright Lights, Big City* that readers learned that the protagonist's name was "Jamie Conway" (a loose homonym of the name "Jay McInerney") and thus had final confirmation that the novel was indeed autobiographical. For personal reasons, however, McInerney steadfastly denies that the novel is autobiographical.

*Commentary*

This first chapter has many details that show why Jamie is in a bad mood for the duration of the novel. For instance, when he leaves the nightclub, the sun has already come up, he doesn't have enough money for a taxi *and* a dog threatens to attack him. He also sees a man dressed as a woman. McInerney thus dramatizes a common refrain of this particular era: "Only in New York!"

## 2. "THE DEPARTMENT OF FACTUAL VERIFICATION"

*Summary*

On Monday, Jamie wakes up late and goes to work. He dreads the ire of his boss, Clara Tillinghast, a strict disciplinarian. Jamie works as a fact checker at a magazine much like *The New Yorker*. He starts double-checking the facts in a piece about French politics. He doesn't know French, even though he said he did when he applied for this job. Jamie would rather work in the fiction department.

Megan Avery offers to help Jamie. Clara tells Jamie that he must finish checking the piece by the end of the day. He says he can, which is a lie. Jamie goes out for lunch. On the street, he buys a fake Cartier watch from a boisterous black man. Back at the office, Jamie has messages from a French person and his brother. He doesn't want to call either one. The editor calls to tell him to check the facts in the piece very carefully. His new watch breaks. He calls the writer of the piece, who isn't much help.

Jamie stays late at work. Tad calls and persuades Jamie to join him and two rich, beautiful women for an evening on the town. He turns in the piece, even though he has not done a good job on it. He remembers that when he first started working at the magazine, he thought he would soon be promoted.

*Commentary*

On his way to work, Jamie reads about the "Coma Baby" in the *New York Post*, a sensationalistic tabloid. This story is a metaphor for Jamie's state of mind since his mother died of cancer. Later in the book, Jamie has a dream in which the Coma Baby says it is content inside the womb. We sympathize with Jamie and forgive his bad attitude and reprobate behavior, because life is indeed more difficult after one leaves the womb.

At least two characters in this chapter are based on real people. "The Druid," the elderly editor of the magazine whom Jamie sees in the hall, is quiet, polite, fussy and mysterious. He is based on William Shawn, the former editor of *The New Yorker*. The writer Richard Fox, who is writing a piece about the magazine, is a sly reference to Tom Wolfe, a writer who wrote a famous article about *The New Yorker* in the 1960s. The story angered Mr. Shawn very much. (The "Fox" and the "Wolf(e)" are similar animals, hence the reference.)

When Jamie is getting lunch, the delicatessen man says that he's fixing a sandwich "just how your mom used to make it." This makes Jamie so angry that he loses his appetite, because he knows that no delicatessen man could ever replace his mother.

## 3. "THE UTILITY OF FICTION"

### Summary
Jamie goes to his apartment. He wants to be a fiction writer but finds it hard to actually sit down and write. He starts to write a letter to Amanda but stops after making some typing errors. Tad arrives, wondering if he has any cocaine, and invites Jamie to go out in search of drugs and women.

Jamie and Tad go to a fashionable restaurant named Odeon, where they meet two fashion models who know Amanda. Tad says she's dead. The four of them go to the bathroom and take cocaine. Then they all go to a nightclub called Heartbreak. Jamie, Tad and a fashion model take some more cocaine in the bathroom. Jamie dances with a woman who feels sorry for him because she thinks Amanda is dead from leukemia. While looking for more cocaine in the ladies' bathroom, Jamie finds the two fashion models having sex with each other.

### Commentary
Cocaine is a white powder made from the coca leaf. Taken internally, it acts first as a stimulant, then as a narcotic, with an intoxicating effect similar to that of hemp. Cocaine is an actual drug, but in the novels of this genre it is also used as a metaphor to criticize the folly of young, wealthy people in certain New York social circles in the late 1980s who pursue fleeting worldly success at the expense of personal growth.

## 4. "A WOMB WITH A VIEW"

### Summary
Megan calls Jamie, reminding him to get out of bed and come to work. Jamie dreads confronting Clara about the shoddy work he did. But Clara does not show up at work that day, so Jamie has more time to fix the French piece.

In the hallway, Jamie runs into Alex Hardy, the magazine's elderly fiction editor emeritus. Hardy invites Jamie to lunch. Hardy drinks a great deal of liquor and doesn't eat much.

## Commentary

When Jamie sees a mannequin that was molded from Amanda's body in a department store window, he is sad. McInerney includes details like this to prove that Jamie has many reasons for his relentless self-pity.

Like Jamie, McInerney worked as a fact checker at *The New Yorker* and was eventually fired. In fact, one reason *Bright Lights, Big City* proved so popular was that many people were interested in what actually happens "behind the scenes" at the secretive *New Yorker*. McInerney shows it to be a place where talent and potential are ignored by the elderly proponents of stultifying tradition. In 1987, McInerney wrote a piece in the *Sunday London Times*, revealing one reason why *The New Yorker* has such a powerful allure to young writers: "Somewhere in the mind of every young man or woman who has ever sent a short story or résumé to the shabby offices on West 43rd Street was the knowledge that J. D. Salinger's *Catcher in the Rye* had first appeared in these pages." Certainly, after McInerney's success with *Bright Lights, Big City*, the editors of *The New Yorker* must have realized what a mistake they had made in firing him.

(Note: Although J. D. Salinger contributed to *The New Yorker*, his novel *The Catcher in the Rye* did not, in fact, appear first in *The New Yorker*.)

# 5. "LES JEUX SONT FAITS"

## Summary

Jamie reminisces about meeting Amanda when they were working in the Midwest. Her mother married a feed salesman who abused Amanda and her mother. When Amanda and Jamie moved to New York, she became a fashion model. Gradually she grew more independent until she left for Paris and telephoned Jamie to say she wasn't returning. She had also met another man, a photographer.

## Commentary

Even though Amanda left Jamie months ago, he still hasn't told anyone about it. Jamie once shouted at one of the window mannequins that looked like Amanda. Jamie's mental instability gives us another reason to pity rather than dislike him.

*Bright Lights, Big City* is a kind of internal monologue in which Jamie repeatedly lists and broods over the many factors in his life which are not going well. After a while, this may seem so tedious and "whiny" to some readers that they will consider putting the book down before finishing it. But due to McInerney's shrewd use of the second-person narrative voice, this is impossible. The protagonist is "you"; if "you" stop reading, "you" are left in limbo. It's probably a better idea to just finish the book.

# 6. "COMA BABY LIVES!"

*Summary*
Jamie's colleagues feel bad for him because he did such a poor job on the French piece. Jamie calls Amanda's modeling agency and finds out that she's doing a show in New York. In the bathroom, he has a conversation with Walter Tyler, the travel editor, who gives him some advice about writing.

Tad leaves a note asking Jamie to entertain his cousin in exchange for some cocaine. Jamie meets Tad's cousin Vicky at a restaurant. Tad gives Jamie a vial of cocaine and then leaves. Jamie and Vicky take a walk, get along well and decide not to meet Tad later.

*Commentary*
McInerney introduces the character Vicky as a foil for Amanda and thus explores his "Madonna/whore" conception of female nature. Vicky is so good and pure that Jamie does not even invite her back to his apartment to try to have sex with her because he wants "to leave his flawless evening intact." We also understand that Vicky is a better person than Amanda because she attends Princeton, an exclusive college in New Jersey, and because she is reading a book of philosophy by Spinoza, a famous hard-to-understand philosopher.

In an earlier scene, Jamie goes to the magazine library and engages the librarian in a discussion of old movies and the alarming increase in indecent language. The librarian's prudish dislike of swear words and sexually explicit writing shows how, in the author's mind, the magazine is behind the times. McInerney's use of swear words and treatment of "inappropriate" topics shows how avant-garde his own writing is and probably explains why he has never had anything published in *The New Yorker*.

# 7. "PYGMIES, FERRETS AND DOG CHOW"

*Summary*
The next morning, Jamie's co-workers tell him that Clara is very angry because the French piece is to be published even though they know there are mistakes in it. Clara calls Jamie into her office and fires him. He goes into the bathroom and takes some cocaine. He agrees to meet Megan for lunch, but then forgets about the date. On the street, Jamie listens to a blues musician.

Later that night, Jamie and Tad return to Clara's office with a ferret, which they plan to leave on Clara's desk as a joke. The ferret bites Jamie. A very drunk Alex Hardy comes into the office. The ferret makes a fuss, and Hardy falls down and loses consciousness. Jamie and Tad go to Tad's apartment, where they bandage Jamie's wounds and take some cocaine. Tad asks rudely about Jamie's evening with Vicky, but Jamie won't say anything.

## Commentary

When Jamie is taking cocaine in the magazine bathroom, he accidentally drops his cocaine in the toilet. This symbolizes that drug abuse can make one's life "go down the toilet." Jamie buys more cocaine from a black youth, who says, "Got coke if you wannit. . . . I'm a businessman. Not a fie-lanthropuss." With this character, McInerney shows that, like Mark Twain and Tama Janowitz, he is a capable satirist of black people. Later in the chapter, when Jamie and Tad drive around in a limousine with a crass Jewish man named Bernie who brags about all the money he has made by being a drug dealer, McInerney shows that, like Charles Dickens and Tama Janowitz, he is a capable satirist of Jews as well.

## 8. "O COUTURE!"

### Summary

Jamie goes to a fashion show, where he has two drinks of vodka and then steals a man's briefcase. To Jamie, the models all look like Amanda. Finally, he sees one that he is sure is Amanda, and he calls out her name. Two security guards escort him from the building because he is a raucous drunk.

### Commentary

The title of this chapter ("O Couture!") is a fashion-industry pun on the French phrase *haut couture*. Like Vladimir Nabokov, McInerney uses puns and wordplay within his narrative for comic and sometimes poignant effect. Some other puns he uses are "A Womb [Room] with a View," an allusion to the E. M. Forster novel, and "All messed [dressed] up and no place to go."

## 9. "LINGUINE AND SYMPATHY"

### Summary

Jamie goes back to the magazine offices, thinking everyone has gone home. Megan is there, and she is mad because he forgot his lunch appointment with her. He finds some cocaine in his desk. He and Megan take the cocaine.

Jamie and Megan go to Megan's apartment. She talks about her own personal problems and cooks dinner. Jamie, drinking heavily, is sexually attracted to Megan. Megan asks about Amanda. Jamie goes into her bathroom and takes one of Megan's Valium sedative pills. He tries to kiss Megan, but she tells him firmly that that is not what he really wants. Jamie loses consciousness.

### Commentary

When Jamie wakes up and goes to the bathroom in Megan's apartment, he falls down and urinates on himself. This scene symbolizes the dangers of drug abuse, in particular the simultaneous ingestion of alcohol and sedatives.

Some may wonder why McInerney deals so frankly with his character's toilet habits and misadventures. One must remember that *Bright Lights, Big City* is a confessional novel, much like Thomas De Quincey's *Confessions of an English Opium-Eater*; its goal is to make the reader know exactly what it was like to have been a member of certain New York social circles in the 1980s. Like many writers, McInerney is only saying what everyone else periodically thinks but refrains from saying or writing about so frankly and at such great length.

## 10. "SOMETIMES A VAGUE NOTION"

### Summary

Jamie wakes up in Megan's empty apartment in the morning. On his way home, he sees his brother Michael sitting on the steps to his apartment. Jamie runs away while Michael runs after him. He walks around uptown, thinking about his life. Then he goes to a bar and meets a girl who asks him if he knows where she can buy some cocaine.

He wakes up the next day in the girl's parents' house in Queens, a middle-class borough of New York City. He goes back to his apartment. His brother shows up, and Jamie considers running away but doesn't. Due to disagreements about Jamie's behavior since their mother's death, Jamie and Michael argue and tussle until Jamie passes out. After Jamie regains consciousness, they take cocaine. Jamie admits that he misses his mother.

### Commentary

Jamie reads in the newspaper that the Coma Baby was delivered but the mother died. This symbolically mirrors the death of Jamie's own mother. The nadir of Jamie's decline is when he wakes up in Queens, an unfashionable part of New York. The "mummies" Jamie sees in the museum, like most things, remind Jamie of his dead "mommy." Jamie literally runs from his brother as a way of figuratively running from his past.

## 11. "THE NIGHT SHIFT"

### Summary

Jamie and Michael go to a restaurant and discuss their mother's death. After they leave, Jamie buys some cocaine, which he and Michael take together. Jamie reminisces about when he went home and his mother was dying. One night she asked about his cocaine and sexual habits. She was experiencing very severe pain but did not want to take morphine because she was enjoying talking to Jamie.

### Commentary

Jamie's memories of his mother's final days are painful, and we now understand why, so far in the narrative, he has been mute on this topic (except for all the recurrent hints). Jamie's mother loved him so deeply and uncon-

ditionally that she refused painkiller injections when he came to visit. She
endured great pain to hear him talk on and on about his life. She could have
taken an injection of morphine so she wouldn't have had to listen to him, but
she didn't. This detail proves his mother's boundless and forgiving love.

## 12. "HOW IT'S GOING"

*Summary*

Tad calls and tells Jamie to come to the Odeon restaurant for a party.
Jamie, Tad and Tad's friend Jimmy Q take a limousine to a party in a loft
apartment. Amanda is at the party, dressed stylishly and standing with a large
Greek man, whom she says is her fiancé. When she asks, "How's it going?"
Jamie has a breakdown, laughing until he can't even see anymore.

When Jamie recovers, he finds a phone and calls Vicky. He tells her that
his mother died a year ago. She is sympathetic. In the morning, Jamie walks
home. He discovers that his nose is bleeding. He smells bread and sees a
bakery. He offers to trade his sunglasses for fresh bread. The bakery man
consents to this deal, and Jamie starts to eat the good-smelling bread right
there.

*Commentary*

This final chapter showcases McInerney's use of the timeless theme *appearance versus reality*. After his laughing fit, Jamie discovers that Amanda's
Greek fiancé is actually a "Dial-a-Hunk" hired escort and that the woman
Stevie, with whom Jamie danced, is in fact a man. These details show that in
certain New York social circles in the 1980s the natural order of things has
been disrupted and perverted. Ultimately, the disparity between appearance
and reality is too much for Jamie; he begins laughing and weeping hysterically,
showing that he is too sensitive to cope with the dislocations of modern life.

At the very end of the book, Jamie realizes that he will "have to go
slowly" and "learn everything all over again." Jamie's trading his sunglasses
for fresh bread symbolizes his rejection of the nightclub life (where vain people
wear sunglasses at night) and his desire to "get back to basics"—such as
fresh bread.

After that, we are to assume, he went home and wrote this novel.

## QUESTIONS FOR REVIEW

1. What do you think is the personal reason McInerney refuses to admit
   that *Bright Lights, Big City* is autobiographical?

2. In McInerney's fiction all women are either "Madonnas" or "whores."
   Agree or disagree, and explain.

3. If you had terminal bone cancer and were in great pain, which would
   you rather do: listen to Jamie Conway talk about his personal problems,
   or take an injection of morphine?

Tama Janowitz was born in San Francisco, California, in 1957. She attended Barnard College. After graduating, she won a series of fellowships and grants. In 1981 Putnam published her first novel, *American Dad*, which received uniformly negative reviews. Putnam rejected her second novel, *A Cannibal in Manhattan*. She received more fellowship and grant money. In 1982, living in New York, she began to write short stories, some of which were published by editor William Shawn in *The New Yorker*. The autobiographical stories of a discontented woman with an uncaring boyfriend contributed to her breakup with her own boyfriend. She became a member of pop artist Andy Warhol's entourage in 1984. In 1985, Crown published *Slaves of New York*, a collection of her short stories. After *Slaves of New York* reached number 15 on the *New York Times* best-seller list, Crown published *A Cannibal in Manhattan* and rereleased *American Dad*, both of which received uniformly negative reviews. *Slaves of New York* was made into an unsuccessful movie in 1989.

# *Slaves of New York* by Tama Janowitz

*(Note:* Slaves of New York *is essentially a novel with two distinct plots, told in alternating, self-contained chapters. Below, the relevant chapters have been grouped by plot and characters to make them more comprehensible.)*

# THE ELEANOR STORIES

## LIST OF CHARACTERS

*Eleanor*

The narrator. She lives with her boyfriend Stash in New York City and hopes to someday design and market unusual jewelry made out of plastic objects. Her parents are divorced.

*Stash*

Eleanor's boyfriend. He is a minor artist, well known in certain New York social circles in the late 1980s.

## 2. "THE SLAVES IN NEW YORK"

*Summary*

Eleanor does Stash's chores, but Stash complains because she is not tidy. At a party, Eleanor meets a novelist named Mikell, who lives with a painter named Millie. Eleanor and Mikell go out for coffee a few days later. Both wish they didn't rely on other people for apartments: Mikell and Millie fight often, as do Eleanor and Stash.

When Eleanor tells Stash she had coffee with Mikell, he is furious at her even though she says it was an innocent, friendly meeting. Eleanor cries. Mikell calls to say that Millie was angry with him also. They decide not to meet again.

Weeks later, Eleanor runs into Mikell by accident, but she hopes he won't call her. She concentrates on being a good roommate and girlfriend to Stash. Eleanor's friend Abby calls and says she wants to move in with a new boyfriend in New York. Eleanor tells her not to.

*Commentary*

Eleanor and Mikell are "slaves" because they rely on their lovers for food, shelter and financial support. They have no independence because they each need a place to live. Eleanor tells her friend that if she moves in with her boyfriend in New York she'll only become a "slave" to him because in New York City the rents are high and there are plenty of available women. Alex Haley wrote about slaves in his book *Roots*, and although those slaves and these "slaves of New York" are different, Janowitz wants us to know that they share the same general alienation and frequent bouts of depression born of limited freedom.

12

The author satirizes the unusual habits of certain New York social circles in the 1980s. For instance, at a party, Eleanor drinks Mexican drinks and discusses China; thus, we see the crazy, upside-down confusion of the post-modern age.

## 7. "SUN POISONING"

*Summary*

Eleanor and Stash go to the tropical island of Haiti for a vacation. Everything goes wrong on the vacation. They have a boring conversation with some unfashionable professional travelers. Stash wears Eleanor's bikini bottom over his head to keep the mosquitoes away. This makes her mad, because he is stretching it out. The next day, he is sick in bed. The day after that, Eleanor and Stash have another bad meal. Eleanor gets sick with sunstroke. The day after that, she goes to the beach wearing long-sleeved clothing and a hat. She says that she's tired of being a woman and that she'd much rather be a man.

*Commentary*

Like McInerney's *Bright Lights, Big City*, "Sun Poisoning" is told in the *second-person* narrative voice. Thus, the reader is thrust into the uncomfortable position of going to Haiti on a vacation that does not go well, and reading about it also. Janowitz is influenced in this story by Malcolm Lowry; her oppressive, nauseating prose reminds one of the environment described in Lowry's novel *Under the Volcano*, which also concerned unpleasant Westerners in a hot, poor country.

Among the things that go wrong on the vacation are: dinner is unpalatable, Stash gets sick, Eleanor gets sick and two teenage boys ignore Eleanor in a bar. The influence of film on Janowitz's work is apparent in this story, with its similarities to *The Out-of-Towners*, *Club Paradise* and *The Heartbreak Kid*.

## 9. "WHO'S ON FIRST?"

*Summary*

Eleanor and Stash play softball with other minor New York artists. She feels out of place at the softball game. She and Stash talk to Mame, who takes heroin, has had some success selling unusual sunglasses in Europe, is pregnant and is unsure about marriage.

Eleanor decides she will only play in the game if she gets a hit during batting practice. She does, and she also gets a hit during the game. A little boy named Mickey won't stop advising Eleanor, so she argues with him. But when Mickey tells Eleanor that she is a good player, she says to him, twice (and both times inscrutably), "You know what's going on."

*Commentary*

At the ballgame, Eleanor frets about playing poorly. She thinks that if she ever gets "job security and/or marital security" she will join the feminist movement. Eleanor's low self-esteem provides a topic for endless rumination and internal monologue. However, when Mickey compliments her, she feels good. We thus understand that Stash and other people in her life have never complimented her enough, and that her problems are other people's fault—a realization common to all novels of this genre.

The title of the story (''Who's on First?'') refers to a famous vaudeville routine by the comedy team Abbott and Costello, in which confusion results due to the imprecise use of ambiguous language.

## 11. "PHYSICS"

### Summary

Eleanor is hit by a car, but she is not hurt. The accident makes her feel very alive. When she gets home, Stash is mad because his art received a negative magazine review. He doesn't want to attend a fancy party at which he will be one of the honored artists. Eleanor and Stash have an argument, and then they make up.

Many exotic and sophisticated people are at the party. Eleanor sits by one, a woman named Samantha, who's wearing a rubber dress. Samantha can't understand why Eleanor lives with Stash, who is not rich and has just received a negative magazine review. Eleanor goes home depressed. Among the things she wishes for are self-confidence, cosmetic nose surgery and a baby. When she asks Stash if he'd like to help her have a baby, he thinks she is crazy or drunk. She walks the dog. When she returns, Stash boasts that he poured a pot of water onto a transvestite and another man who were necking in the bushes. This makes Eleanor mad. She suddenly wishes she could go back to high school and study physics, which she thinks would help her understand life better.

### Commentary

After the fancy party, Samantha and her stylish friends drive by in a limousine and ask Eleanor to join them. Eleanor declines and is left standing on the curb holding a glass of champagne. Like Henry James and F. Scott Fitzgerald, Janowitz uses *material objects* to illuminate social and emotional states. Eleanor's glass of champagne represents her taste of ''the good life,'' while the departing limousine represents the ''life in the fast lane'' that is passing her by.

## 14. "SPELLS"

### Summary

At Daria's birthday party, Eleanor is jealous when Stash talks to Daria, so Eleanor talks to Daria's boyfriend, Simon. Later, Stash says he likes Daria's art and will help her meet Victor, who runs a gallery. Eleanor feels dizzy and lies down on the street. Stash wants her to go to the hospital emergency room, but she doesn't want to.

A few days later, Eleanor, Stash, Daria and Simon go to a horror movie. Eleanor feels inferior to Daria, but after realizing that Daria too might feel inferior, she feels better, until Stash ignores her. After the movie they all go to a party. Eleanor feels sick again and almost faints.

The next day, Eleanor goes to a clinic, where the doctor tells her she has a fainting virus. At home, she eats a whole bottle of ketchup and gets angry because Stash is with Daria, whose dog has died. When Stash gets home, she tells him that the doctor spent five hours examining her breasts, and he gets angry.

*Commentary*

Eleanor's physical nausea mirrors her emotional instability, a condition also suffered by the narrator of McInerney's *Bright Lights, Big City*, Clay in Bret Easton Ellis's *Less Than Zero* and Mgungu in Janowitz's own *A Cannibal in Manhattan*. But unlike the nausea felt by Ellie in McCloy's *Velocity*, Lauren in Ellis's *The Rules of Attraction* and Alison in McInerney's *Story of My Life*, Eleanor's nausea does not foreshadow a pregnancy and subsequent abortion.

# 16. "FONDUE"

*Summary*

Eleanor makes cheese fondue and cries. She remembers having lunch with Lord Simeon when she was studying in England. A few days before the lunch, she dyed her hair green and couldn't wash all the color out. At lunch, Eleanor felt that she didn't know the proper way to behave, even though Lord Simeon was very polite and attentive.

Eleanor calls her mother and says that she is moving out of Stash's apartment. Her mother is supportive and understanding, but Eleanor cries anyway. Eleanor and her mother discover that they've both eaten the same brand of fondue recently by coincidence. Eleanor says she later saw Lord Simeon deliver a speech in America, but he didn't remember her.

*Commentary*

On her way to see Lord Simeon, Eleanor saw an empty glass case with a sign that said: "Here Rest the Mortal Remains of Jeremy Bentham." This detail is mentioned repeatedly in the story. Jeremy Bentham was an eighteenth-century philosopher who espoused the concept of utilitarianism, which sought to define "the greatest good for the greatest number of people." Because Janowitz's characters embody a notion of individual liberty taken to a radical, modern extreme, the allusion to Bentham is ironic and meaningful.

"Fondue" is the sixth of eight stories about Eleanor's low self-esteem, emotional discomfort and apparent inability to master minor points of social etiquette.

# 19. "PATTERNS"

*Summary*
    Eleanor has broken up with Stash and moved into her own apartment.
She missed him for a while, but then something he said about their relationship
based on something he saw on TV made her not miss him anymore. She writes
a letter to Wilfredo, a fashion designer she once met, and they meet for dinner.
She likes Wilfredo, and he likes her jewelry. She thinks she is in love again.
    She goes to Wilfredo's apartment for a dinner party. The couples are all
men. Eleanor talks about how she doesn't think women's independence is all
it's made out to be. Hank and Mike have a spat and then leave. Eleanor spends
the night with Wilfredo and leaves the next morning very happy.
    Wilfredo does not call. Eleanor reads books about how to make men fall
in love, asks her mother and a psychic for advice and walks around Wilfredo's
neighborhood.

*Commentary*
    The reader understands that Wilfredo is homosexual. Eleanor does not.
This is called *dramatic irony*.

# 21. "MATCHES"

*Summary*
    Eleanor decides to give a party, but few of the preparations go right. She
goes for a walk and meets a friendly man named Jan. They ride on his motorcycle, and she invites him to her party. She runs into two married men she
knows, and she invites them to the party.
    At the party, all but one of the guests are men. Jan arrives with a suitcase,
saying his girlfriend kicked him out and that he thought he'd stop by the party
before he goes to get a hotel room. A table falls down. Eleanor thinks the
party was a failure, but her friends assure her it wasn't any worse than any
other party.

*Commentary*
    This final story in the Eleanor cycle brings no conclusions or changes in
Eleanor. Like Thomas Pynchon's *The Crying of Lot 49*, the Eleanor stories
avoid *closure*. Like real life, they just keep going on and on in the same way
without much change.

# QUESTION FOR REVIEW

1. Like Dickens, Janowitz writes frequently about coincidence: Eleanor
   and her mother both eating cheese fondue in different states, for instance, and Eleanor meeting Lord Simeon again. In light of the subtle
   but resonant logic behind most of these coincidences, what do you
   make of Eleanor's boyfriend wearing her bikini pants on his head and
   then getting sick the next day?

# THE MARLEY MANTELLO STORIES

## LIST OF CHARACTERS

**Marley Mantello**
 A 29-year-old art school graduate living in New York City. He is a painter, and he thinks he is a genius. His father is dead.

**Ginger**
 Marley's art dealer.

**Sherman**
 A painter friend of Marley's.

**Lacey**
 Sherman's, and then Marley's, girlfriend.

**Marley's sister**
 She committed suicide.

## 5. "LIFE IN THE PRE-CAMBRIAN ERA"

*Summary*
 At the bank, people stare at Marley because of his eccentric clothes. Marley's mother visits. She wants him to do something more productive with his life. Marley's mother has had a hard life; her father disowned her when she became pregnant, and her husband left her and then died. Now she thinks she is pregnant by a college professor. She leaves.
 Marley gets excited thinking that he might have a little brother. He meets a friend named Larry in the supermarket. Larry is dying of AIDS. Marley goes for a walk and gives an offering "to the gods" by throwing his ice cream in the river. Then he cuts his hair with fingernail clippers.

*Commentary*
 Marley suffers from *delusions of grandeur*, a psychological phenomenon in which a person believes that they are more powerful or more talented then they actually are. The uncanny accuracy with which Janowitz depicts this state of mind shows that her knowledge of the condition goes far beyond that of a mere observer.

## 10. "TURKEY TALK"

*Summary*
 Marley's art dealer, Ginger, takes him to the home of an art collector named Chuck Dade Dolger. Chuck cooks lots of food and makes Marley eat

it. Chuck talks about how he became a self-made man. Marley realizes that Ginger and Chuck are going steady. Ginger tries to persuade Marley not to mention his idea for a chapel that will celebrate Christ as a woman, as she thinks it might put Chuck off buying one of Marley's paintings.

Marley walks Chuck's dog, then leaves. On the street, Marley becomes very happy when he realizes that he is once again hungry. He has a slice of bad pizza and tells the counterman his plans for the chapel of Christ as a woman.

### Commentary
Marley's encounter with a wealthy person represents a clash of two different social worlds. Marley values his ideas and artistic integrity, while the fat, overindulging Chuck Dade Dolger values money and material belongings. Marley prizes his art too much to "sell out to the Establishment." By using *dramatic irony*, Janowitz mocks and satirizes Marley's self-righteous and financially self-destructive idealism.

## 13. "IN AND OUT OF THE CAT BAG"

### Summary
Marley is about to be evicted from his apartment. He runs into his sculptor friend Sherman, who is on crutches. Sherman is angry at Marley, because Marley told Sherman's girlfriend Lacey that he is successful, thus insinuating that Sherman is not. Sherman and Lacey are no longer going steady. Marley invites Sherman over and thinks about how they were once friends, even though Marley has always considered Sherman an inferior artist.

Marley discovers a stray cat in his apartment bathroom. Sherman arrives with some liquor. The landlord reminds him he will be evicted soon. Marley makes bad pancakes. Sherman thinks Marley's ideas for paintings are behind the times. Marley gets a phone call from a woman saying that she's coming over to seduce him. That woman is Lacey.

### Commentary
While talking to Sherman, Marley holds forth on how insects are stronger than humans, and how insects will rule the world after nuclear war. This is just one example of the artistic manifesto Janowitz proposes with her fiction: that fiction need not be an elite, high-minded branch of the culture and that it should incorporate themes drawn from old television shows, the world of advertising, cocktail-party banter and the routines of second-rate comedians.

## 17. "ON AND OFF THE AFRICAN VELDT"

### Summary
Marley takes some new paintings to his dealer, Ginger. He takes the subway to the museum, where he looks at animals of the African veldt. That night, he goes to the opening of a show of Sherman's paintings. Sherman has

18

been drinking liquor. Marley and Lacey go to dinner at a Japanese restaurant with Sherman, Sherman's girlfriend Willow and Borali, Sherman's dealer. Marley asks everyone to name the most disgusting meal they've ever had. Borali talks about eating whole fried little birds once, and about watching people eat the brains out of a live monkey's skull with spoons. Sherman is angry because Marley has ruined the dinner by bringing Lacey and initiating an unpleasant conversation.

### Commentary

After the dinner, Marley and Lacey eat at a McDonald's. Marley says he loves to eat meat that's almost raw and bloody. This meal foreshadows Mgungu the cannibal's meal at the same place in Janowitz's subsequent novel, *A Cannibal in Manhattan*. Janowitz seems almost obsessed with this famous fast-food hamburger restaurant and the food it serves.

## 20. "ODE TO THE HEROINE OF THE FUTURE"

### Summary

Marley tells of his sister who committed suicide. He compares her to the heroes of ancient Greece. Marley's sister used drugs and liquor excessively.

Marley's sister once described a lesbian experience she'd had. After her divorce she accidentally walked into a lesbian bar, but decided to stay. An older lesbian woman dressed like a man came into the bar. She and Marley's sister danced together, but then the lesbian woman's lesbian friend slapped Marley's sister. Marley's sister and the first lesbian woman went into the bathroom. Marley's sister took the woman's clothes off, bit her nipple, burned her side with a cigarette and then ran out. The next day Marley's sister ran into the woman in a grocery store. The woman had been calling her ever since.

Eventually, Marley's sister committed suicide because she had been taking a lot of cocaine and her European friends wouldn't give her any more. Marley wishes they hadn't published the grotesque picture of his dead sister's corpse in the newspaper.

### Commentary

Marley's braggadocio makes him interesting, but almost unbearable to listen to or, more literally, to keep reading. But in this final story in the Marley Mantello cycle, we learn that Marley's younger sister fell in with a bad crowd and committed suicide. Thus, finally, we have a reason to pity Marley, which makes it easier to listen to his story, which is now over.

## QUESTION FOR REVIEW

1. If a real-life Marley Mantello approached you on the street and began telling you the story of his life, would you listen? If you *would* listen

to him for quite a while, why? If someone you don't know then asked you to answer a question about what Marley had said, would you answer?

# INCIDENTAL CHAPTERS

## 1. "MODERN SAINT #271"

*Summary*
The narrator is a Jewish woman from the South who has become a prostitute in New York. Her pimp, Bob, is a writer and heroin addict. Her father, a wealthy automobile dealer, disowned her because she kept getting expelled from private schools for misbehaving with men. She thinks she could write a book about being a prostitute, but she gives all her good ideas to Bob.

*Commentary*
This story is rife with *difficult religious symbolism*. For instance, the narrator's work in New York reminds her of being in a convent, and the moon reminds her of her destiny and of holy water.

Like Charles Dickens and George Orwell, Janowitz writes frankly about the dark underside of urban life. The detailed descriptive passage about varieties of the human penis (page 1 in the paperback edition) may be of particular interest to some readers.

## 3. "ENGAGEMENTS"

*Summary*
Cora, a graduate student in feminist criticism at Yale University, meets Ray at a school party. She doesn't really like him, but she accompanies him to New York to meet his wealthy parents and accepts many presents from him. Cora's older sister died of leukemia when they were young. Cora's classes confuse her. She leaves Yale and moves in with her mother in Southampton, a wealthy resort town on Long Island.
Ray visits and asks Cora to marry him. She declines. Cora tries to rent a nice apartment she looked at before but discovers that Ray has bought it and modernized it, thus ruining it. She sees Ray's father on TV selling mattresses, which is how he became rich.

*Commentary*
Like Flaubert's *Madame Bovary*, "Engagements" uses precise detail and observation to tell the story of an ordinary woman at a certain time and place—in this case, certain Northeastern collegiate social circles in the 1980s. Janowitz achieves a Flaubertian verisimilitude by noting that it is difficult to find a good, inexpensive apartment in New York City. Like Eleanor, Cora is a slave to high apartment prices. She is one of the Slaves of New York.

# 4. "YOU AND THE BOSS"

*Summary*
This story, like "Sun Poisoning," is told in the second-person narrative voice. The protagonist loves the famous pop musician Bruce Springsteen. She gives Springsteen's wife a lobotomy and then takes her place. Springsteen doesn't notice because he spends most of his time rehearsing with his combo and only likes to have sex in a car parked behind a factory. Springsteen spends his free time magically healing sick senior citizens. The protagonist discovers she is pregnant. She flees to Hollywood and sends Springsteen's real wife back to live with Springsteen. The protagonist takes over Springsteen's real wife's job at a wax museum. She feels Springsteen's child kicking in her womb.

*Commentary*
Bruce Springsteen is a popular musician in real life. His nickname is "The Boss"—hence the title of the story. His professional reputation is that of a journeyman troubadour or "rock poet." Like E. L. Doctorow's *Ragtime*, "You and the Boss" uses a real-life person as a fictional character. Springsteen is often criticized for making money by writing songs about people who don't have very much money, and Janowitz confirms this thesis by using trenchant fictional satire.

# 6. "CASE HISTORY #4: FRED"

*Summary*
Fred, a musician, likes to approach women on the street, say he is a millionaire and offer to take them to Tiffany's, an expensive jewelry store. He takes one woman there but says he's forgotten his credit card. The experience makes him feel very alive. Eventually the people at Tiffany's begin to recognize Fred, and he is arrested. He promises never to return. He stops approaching women, and his musical compositions lose their "old zip and snap."

*Commentary*
Fred is a new and improved version of the character Holly Golightly in Truman Capote's famous novella *Breakfast at Tiffany's*. Like Golightly, Fred seeks to create a new identity for himself through use of fantasy, lying and the diamond counter at Tiffany's.

In the story, Fred thinks about the German philosopher Nietzsche, who was raped by a nymphomaniac countess dressed as a man, and how this affected Nietzsche's famous philosophical idea of the "Superman." Alone among modern novelists, Janowitz has reconciled the ideas of Truman Capote and Friedrich Nietzsche by referring to them in the same story.

# 8. "SNOWBALL"

*Summary*
Victor is a gallery owner whose business is failing. He competes with Betty Brown, a younger gallery owner. He lives with Sistina, a fashion model, whose cat, Snowball, Victor is allergic to. Snowball bites Victor. An artist gets angry at Victor. Victor's secretary is surly to him. Victor asks Betty Brown to dinner, but she laughs at him. Victor forgets Sistina's birthday. Sistina moves in with Victor's photographer neighbor. Snowball jumps on Victor and claws his back.

*Commentary*
The themes of free will, destiny and bad luck are explored. Victor is one of the few Janowitz characters over the age of 35, so his life is falling apart. The cat is a symbol for how, when everything seems to be going wrong, another thing will go wrong. American businessmen call this *Murphy's Law*. The ancient Greeks called it *tragedy*.

# 12. "LUNCH INVOLUNTARY"

*Summary*
The unnamed narrator recites a day-by-day menu for a week's worth of meals, and then recites it slightly differently. She eats in a cafeteria. She thinks she's being served less food lately. Eventually, she is served only one pea for lunch. One day, the cashier refuses to accept her meal ticket, and the narrator realizes that everyone else is using a different-color ticket.

*Commentary*
In "Lunch Involuntary," Janowitz dabbles in a terse surreal monologue reminiscent of Eugene Ionesco, Joseph Heller, Donald Barthelme and various undergraduate literary journals. The narrator is confused; readers who finish the story will sympathize. The obsolete green meal ticket is a metaphor for the fleeting nature of fame, a recurrent Janowitz theme. Some have called this story one of the ten or twenty most interesting pieces ever to appear in *Lo Spazio Umano*.

# 15. "THE NEW ACQUAINTANCES"

*Summary*
Clarence, a wealthy, eccentric college student, lives with Inez, a girl he met on the street. Clarence insists that Inez will eventually marry him. Inez finds a little boy named Andrew beating a cat and brings the boy and the cat to Clarence's home. Clarence is failing all his classes.

Clarence and Inez have dinner with Clarence's wealthy parents, who drink a great deal of liquor. Inez tells them that she was raped when she was 16.

Back at Clarence's house, Andrew tells them that his mother is raising him as the second Messiah. Ferenc arrives to deliver a pizza. Inez leaves with Andrew. Clarence goes to the closet to feed a slice of pizza to the unspecified yowling creature inside.

### Commentary
The writer William Burroughs (like Janowitz a bohemian resident of Manhattan's Lower East Side) pioneered the literary technique of writing down random sentences, cutting them into strips, jumbling them and then committing them to paper in whatever order they came out.

## 18. "CASE HISTORY #15: MELINDA"

### Summary
Melinda, a bartender, owns an apartment she bought with insurance money from a taxi accident that ended her dancing career. She takes crippled animals home with her. She thinks that when she meets the right man, he will not be disgusted by the odor and mess of the animals in her apartment.

Melinda takes home a young man named Chicho and cares for him. She contracts a rare bone disease from drinking water a rat has urinated in. She is expected to die, but recovers. She returns home to find that Chicho has redone her apartment, gotten rid of all the animals and is having sex with her best friend. She throws him out, collects more animals and continues her life as before, "neither joyful nor despairing."

### Commentary
The unavoidable dangers of urban life are symbolized by Chicho's betrayal and by the rat urine. Melinda tries to insulate herself from the former by surrounding herself with animals, which are capable of unconditional love, but she cannot avoid the latter. Life, Janowitz is saying, is full of difficult choices.

## 22. "KURT AND NATASHA, A RELATIONSHIP"

### Summary
Kurt is a handsome German artist who is well known in certain New York social circles. He meets Natasha, invites her home and then tapes her up and has sex with her. Natasha moves in. Kurt makes her wear handcuffs, skimpy clothing and other decadent sexual paraphernalia while she cleans the apartment. Soon, she too becomes well known in certain New York social circles.

Natasha's sister comes to visit. Kurt notices that he has become physically smaller than Natasha. He tapes up Natasha's sister and has sex with her. He thinks about leaving Natasha, but then thinks that there are perhaps more sisters at home.

Kurt throws Natasha out, and she takes up with a successful artist who knows that Kurt is a "has-been." Kurt goes to a therapist who says that Kurt both adores and fears women. A while later, Kurt sees Natasha at a party. She is now physically huge, but not in an obese way. He takes her into the bathroom and tries to bind her with tape, but she tapes him up instead.

### Commentary

Physical size is a metaphor for the power that comes with fame in certain New York circles. When Kurt tapes up Natasha or her sister or makes Natasha wear handcuffs while she cleans the apartment, he is making them his slaves. He is making them Slaves of New York.

## SUGGESTIONS FOR FURTHER READING

"Page Six" item (*New York Post*, December 18, 1985): Janowitz and photographer Patrick McMullan seen together at nightclubs BeBop Cafe, Kamikaze, TNR, Area and the Saint. All in one night.

"Page Six" item (*New York Post*, August 19, 1986): Janowitz gives a dinner party for eighty people, including Matt Dillon, Iman and Andy Warhol. She gives out novelty shop gag items as party favors.

"Page Six" item (*New York Post*, November 3, 1986): A new short story by Janowitz is to appear as a Christmas window display in a men's clothing store but is rejected because she will not eliminate references to drug abuse and prostitution.

"Page Six" item (*New York Post*, November 26, 1986): Janowitz and her friends make a scene at the Tavern on the Green restaurant, taking posed photos for her upcoming novel *A Cannibal in Manhattan*.

"Page Six" item (*New York Post*, December 19, 1986): Janowitz meets author Tom Wolfe (who had, unlike historian Arthur Schlesinger, Jr., declined to appear in a Rose's Lime Juice ad with her) at Le Cirque.

"Page Six" item (*New York Post*, May 7, 1987): Tama moves from the West Village to the Upper West Side, taking her dogs Lulu and Beep-Beep with her.

"The Night of Tama Janowitz: Manhattan Writer Takes a Whirl at LA Club Scene" (*Los Angeles Times*, June 22, 1987): Account of Janowitz's publicity party for paperback edition of *Slaves of New York* at Vertigo nightclub in Los Angeles.

"The Evening Hours" (*New York Times*, July 17, 1987): Janowitz judges a pastry and cake competition at Nicole, a restaurant in New York.

"Page Six" item (*New York Post*, August 18, 1987): Janowitz receives free samples of dog perfume from Le Chien Dog Salon; tries the perfume on her dogs, self.

"Page Six" item (*New York Post*, October 21, 1987): At a luncheon, Janowitz tells how she was burglarized recently. The burglar took nothing of much value: orange juice, a cassette player and a copy of *A Cannibal in Manhattan*.

"Advertisements for Themselves" (*The New Yorker*, October 26, 1987): Terrence Rafferty discusses the novelists of the genre.

"Style '87: Dash and Trash" (*People Weekly*, November 16, 1987): Janowitz helps judge which famous people were the best- or worst-dressed of 1987.

"The Wilton North Report" (failed television show on the Fox Television Network, December 1987 to January 1988): Janowitz appeared as a roving correspondent.

"Page Six" item (*New York Post*, June 16, 1988): Janowitz begins dating Adam Coleman Howard, the actor who plays the character based on Tama's former boyfriend in the movie version of *Slaves of New York*.

"Page Six" item (*New York Post*, July 30, 1988): Janowitz covers the Democratic Convention in Atlanta for *Spin*, a pop music fan magazine. A group of young Hollywood actors (including Rob Lowe, Ally Sheedy, Leif Garrett and Judd Nelson) are mean to Janowitz because they think she is writing a critical article about them. Janowitz's spokesperson explains that Janowitz had no intention of writing a critical article, but that because the young actors were unkind to her, she probably will. Later, she does.

"Page Six" item (*New York Post*, October 25, 1988): Tama appears in a Marvel Comics *Spiderman* issue as herself, "an important serious writer."

*Women's Wear Daily* (November 1, 1988): Janowitz models clothes for designer Betsey Johnson in an amateur fashion show.

"Page Six" item (*New York Post*, November 14, 1988): Janowitz is seen at El Morocco restaurant with Tim Hunt, a "dashing Brit who works for the Warhol Foundation."

*New York Woman* (January 1989): "Loose Lips" column reports that Janowitz has been seen at "not one but two dinner parties with dirt-encrusted fingernails."

"Page Six" item (*New York Post*, January 18, 1989): Janowitz explains her dirty fingernails by making a joke about homeless people: "I and two of my close friends have been working to clean the subway station where we sleep. There was no hot water and someone stole the soap."

"Page Six" item (*New York Post*, March 3, 1989): A cocktail party celebrating the opening of the *Slaves of New York* movie is planned at the Bloomingdale's *Slaves of New York* clothing boutique. A dinner party at M.K. discothèque is to follow. Two nights later, another cocktail party is planned at a gallery showing the work of artists featured in the film. A party at the World discothèque will follow.

# BIOGRAPHICAL NOTE

    Bret Easton Ellis was born in Los Angeles in 1964. He attended Bennington, an exclusive, progressive, expensive arts-oriented college in Vermont, where he studied fiction writing under the best-selling non-fiction writer Joe McGinnis. McGinnis sent a draft of Ellis's *Less Than Zero* to an editor at Simon & Schuster, a New York publishing house. *Less Than Zero* was published in 1985, while Ellis was still a 21-year-old college senior. After graduation in 1986, Ellis planned to start a rock-and-roll combo in New York but did not. *Less Than Zero* was made into an unsuccessful movie in 1987. Ellis's second novel, *The Rules of Attraction*, was published in 1987 and received uniformly negative reviews. Ellis lives in New York.

# *Less Than Zero* by Bret Easton Ellis

## LIST OF CHARACTERS

### Clay
    An 18-year old who attends an exclusive college in New England and returns to his home in California during Christmas vacation. His grandmother is dead.

### Blair
    Clay's high school girlfriend, who still lives in Los Angeles.

### Julian, Rip, Spin, Finn, Kim, Daniel, Derf
    Friends of Clay's.

26

# I–IX

Summary

Clay returns to Los Angeles. Blair picks him up at the airport and says that people are afraid to merge on freeways in the city. At home Clay lies down, feeling ill. He watches television and tries to call Julian.

Clay and Daniel go to Blair's party. People think Clay looks pale and unhealthy. Clay looks for Rip, his drug dealer. Blair's father, a homosexual movie producer, is talking to a young actor. Blair's father's boyfriend Jared is there also. This makes Blair's mother nervous. No one knows where Julian is, but they say he's in a bad way lately. Clay and Daniel go to the Polo Lounge, a restaurant in the Beverly Hills Hotel frequented by people in the movie business, and Daniel says that he wants to go back—he doesn't know where to, just back.

Clay and his mother have an awkward conversation in an unidentified restaurant. His mother drinks a lot of wine. Clay and Trent go to a restaurant shaped like a train to meet Julian, who is to bring some cocaine for Trent. When Julian does not show up, they look for him at an arcade and then a fast-food chain restaurant called Fatburger. Then they go to a nightclub called the Edge. Trent gives Clay a Quaalude tranquilizer pill. They find Daniel and Blair. Daniel is very drunk, but they make sure he gets to his car safely. Clay drives Blair home, and she asks why he never called her while he was away at school.

Clay goes to a shopping center with his mother and two sisters. He sits in a bar at La Scala Boutique and drinks wine. While they're driving home, his sisters tease him about always locking the door to his room. He tells them he does it because his sisters once stole some cocaine from him. Clay goes to a psychoanalyst but lies to him.

Commentary

"People are afraid to merge in Los Angeles" is a phrase that resonates in Clay's mind throughout the novel. Its metaphorical meaning is that people in Los Angeles are afraid to connect with each other, to be open and honest, to really get to know and like other people.

Clay's pale skin tone—like Hester Prynne's scarlet "A" in Hawthorne's *The Scarlet Letter*—symbolizes that his going to an exclusive college in the East has made him an outsider back home. In a 1986 interview, Bret Easton Ellis said, "I am part of this lost generation. Being a writer or being an artist and commenting on it doesn't exclude you from the group. You are still part of that thing of people." Like Ellis, Clay is a detached observer of—and at the same time, a member of—this particular thing of people.

# X–XVII

Summary

Clay meets Blair, Alana and Kim at a restaurant named Du-Par's. Blair says that Muriel has anorexia and is in the hospital. The girls discuss who is having sex with whom, and Clay tries to remember if he had sex with a particular person. They discuss a girl who likes having sex with two fellows at once and who retains a bisexual black boyfriend to expedite this.

Clay and Trent go to Kim's party. Julian is there. Blair gives Clay a scarf. Clay meets Rip, and they take some cocaine. Clay buys some cocaine from Rip. Clay goes to the bathroom to take some more cocaine, but Trent tells him that Julian, Kim and Derf are inside having sex. Clay and Trent sit in Trent's car and take some more cocaine. Clay goes home and has sex with a fellow named Griffin.

Clay wakes up in the morning, takes some cocaine, swims in the pool, eats an orange, takes some more cocaine, watches television and then drives to meet his father for lunch. He sees a billboard that says "Disappear Here." This phrase resonates in his mind. Clay meets his father in a fancy office building. Clay's father works in the film industry and has just had a hair transplant and cosmetic surgery on his face. Clay's father asks him if he would like to go to Palm Springs. Clay remembers a time when he skipped school and drove to his family's other house, in Palm Springs. Clay cried because the house was in a state of disrepair. He thought about the happy weekends he'd spent there when he was younger.

### Commentary

The billboard slogan "Disappear Here" is another phrase that resonates in Clay's mind. It has an infinite number of symbolic meanings, but two seem particularly important. One is that the possibility of suicide or death is frequently on Clay's mind. The other is that Clay is torn between two worlds—the world of school back east and the decadent world of Los Angeles. Also, school back east represents maturity and adulthood, while Los Angeles represents the innocent, carefree days of childhood.

When Clay remembers his happy childhood visits to Palm Springs, we realize that it is not his fault he has become jaded and overindulgent; it is society's fault. The crumbling house symbolizes the inexorable triumph of time over youth.

Clay's father's cosmetic surgery symbolizes the unnatural, narcissistic and ultimately destructive tampering with the natural order of things that makes Los Angeles decadent.

# XVIII–XXX

### Summary

Clay visits Muriel in the hospital, and they have an awkward conversation. Two men in a car follow Clay around, and he thinks they are "insane fags [homosexuals]." Clay has an awkward conversation with Julian in a restaurant called Cafe Casino. Julian has dropped out of school and looks unkempt. Clay goes to Rip's apartment. Rip's boyfriend Spin is lying naked on the bed using cocaine, and a 16-year-old boy is getting dressed to leave. Clay buys some cocaine from Rip.

Clay goes to Trent's house, where Trent is trying to buy some cocaine over the telephone. Clay says he is not going out with Blair anymore. They have an awkward conversation with Trent's mother. Clay and Blair go to Daniel's party. Clay takes Blair home. They have sex and then an awkward conversation.

Clay remembers going with Blair to his parents' beach house in Monterey. They had sex repeatedly and drank lots of champagne. The more they drank, the less fun they had, until Clay realized it was time to leave. Clay goes to a fast-food chain restaurant named Sambo's. Clay buys a pornographic magazine. He goes home, watches TV and thinks about the billboard slogan "Disappear Here." The next day, Daniel calls. He has taken a bad Quaalude tranquilizer pill. A girl he was having sex with at college is probably pregnant, and her parents just got divorced.

Clay goes to a "square" restaurant named Chasen's with his parents and sisters. His father has been drinking a lot of champagne. They all have an awkward conversation. Clay thinks about the major themes of the novel: people afraid to merge, "Disappear Here," and so on. He wonders if Julian is "for sale." On the way to a bar, they see a car accident. Clay remembers one Christmas in Palm Springs when it was particularly hot and he smoked marijuana.

### Commentary

In this section, Ellis updates themes popularized by F. Scott Fitzgerald and Ernest Hemingway. Clay sees a restaurant patron speak rudely to a waitress because the waitress lives in "the Valley," an unfashionable middle-class part of the Los Angeles area. In Ellis's Los Angeles—as in Fitzgerald's East Egg and West Egg (in *The Great Gatsby*)—the neighborhood in which a person lives can be cause for social prejudice.

In a 1986 interview, Ellis compared his generation to the "Lost Generation" of Hemingway and Fitzgerald: "Whatever is considered 'lost,' this time is different. Instead of drinking a lot or just wandering around Europe, the specifics of, say, *Less Than Zero* are more drug oriented. . . ." Ellis's "Lost Generation" faces an even bleaker world than that of Hemingway and Fitzgerald. In Hemingway and Fitzgerald's age, the shadow of an unimaginably bloody world war left a whole generation spiritually scarred. Similarly, in Ellis's time, drugs and money to buy them are all too available, and music-video television has stunted the intellectual and emotional growth of a whole young generation.

# XXXI–XLI

### Summary

Blair tells Clay she still likes him and that they should not break up. Clay looks at old photos of him and Blair, and this makes him sad. On Christmas day, Clay takes some cocaine. After Christmas, Clay goes to a "beach club" with Blair, Alana, Kim, Rip and Griffin. Blair says Muriel is out of the hospital. Clay takes a Nembutal tranquilizer pill.

Clay sees his sisters watching a pornographic film. One of them says she doesn't like the part where the male partner ejaculates. Clay remembers a gruesome car accident he once saw in Palm Springs. After that he started collecting news clippings about other acts of violence. Trent tells Clay that some people he knows think there is a werewolf around. Clay watches religious television and looks out his window for werewolves.

After Clay and Blair have sex, they go to a party at Kim's house. Kim says that Julian is having sex with a number of lawyers from Beverly Hills. Clay sees a dog eat a cigarette butt. A young actress says that former Los Angeles County Coroner Thomas Noguchi might come to this party. When they discover Muriel injecting heroin in the bathroom, they watch her for a while, and then the party winds down.

Clay watches more religious TV. He goes to the famous Chinese Theater to meet Julian, but Julian doesn't show up. Clay goes to Trent's house and talks to Blair, who says that Julian wants to see him. Clay drives around looking for Julian. He goes to a party, where he finds out that Julian owes many people money. Clay has an awkward conversation with Julian at a shopping mall. Julian wants to borrow money from Clay. He says he needs the money for a girl to have an abortion.

Clay buys some cocaine from Rip. Then they go to a Japanese sushi restaurant in Studio City. They discuss popular music—specifically, which performers are fashionable and which are not. Clay meets Blair at Kim's house. They go to a horror movie, which Clay finds boring.

***Commentary***

That Clay's young sisters are allowed to watch a pornographic film is an indictment of their parents' permissive social values. Clay's sister's aversion to ejaculation scenes shows how these graphic sex movies are warping her: she now dislikes ejaculation, which is a natural and generally desirable component of the sexual process. The dog who eats a cigarette butt is a symbol for the fact that Los Angeles is such a decadent environment that even the animals behave in a sick, unnatural way.

The expected appearance of Los Angeles County Coroner Thomas Noguchi at Kim's party is a macabre foreshadowing of death by unnatural causes.

# L–LXI

***Summary***

Trent calls Clay to say he is upset because he does not have any cocaine and is having girl problems. Trent and Clay go to a movie and smoke marijuana. The next day, Clay goes to Julian's house to give him the money. Clay and Rip have lunch at a restaurant named La Scala Boutique. They discuss the unseasonably hot weather.

Clay, Kim and Blair go to a nightclub called the Edge. Clay meets a person, and they take cocaine together. Clay meets with his psychoanalyst, who wants Clay to help him write a screenplay. Clay goes to Trent's apartment. Rip, Chris and Atiff are there. They discuss a person who used to be "normal" before he started taking heroin. Clay says, "What does normal mean to you?"

Later, Clay lies around his room thinking about his dreams in which he sinks into the ground. He keeps getting phone calls from someone who doesn't say anything. Clay, Trent and Blair take some cocaine and then go to a Hollywood restaurant named Spago. Clay tells Trent that he and Blair aren't dating anymore. Then they all go to a nightclub named After Hours. Blair meets Rip and they go somewhere together. Clay goes into the bathroom and stares at himself in the mirror instead of taking cocaine. Clay goes home with a girl who makes him wear sunglasses and masturbate while she masturbates using some suntan lotion.

Clay goes to his psychoanalyst, sneezes blood and cries. The psychoanalyst tells Clay he will be fine, but Clay is not so sure. Clay remembers a holiday in Palm Springs. His grandparents were there, and they discussed death.

### Commentary

When Clay's friends discuss a friend who was "normal" before he started taking heroin, Clay asks, "What does normal mean to you?" Rather than conforming to the ideas of his peers, Clay rebels against their world-view by asking this question. Indeed, what is "normal" in a society gone mad?

The unseasonably hot weather—like the dog that eats a cigarette—is a symbol of the apocalyptic decline of Los Angeles. Ellis has said that the writer Joan Didion's style greatly influenced his own. She too has written of the unseasonably hot weather in Los Angeles, and although she has never written of a cigarette-eating dog, Ellis's debt to her is obvious.

Clay's dreams tell us that he feels as if he's sinking into the ground, probably figuratively.

# LXII–LXXI

### Summary

Clay, Rip and Spin go to the Hard Rock Cafe restaurant in Beverly Hills. Rip and Spin say that Julian is always "strung out," and that he sells inferior quality cocaine and sometimes heroin to high school students. They smoke marijuana while they drive to the house of a person named "Dead." Dead is a 40-year-old man, and his house is full of young boys in bathing suits. They buy some cocaine from Dead. They take the cocaine in Rip's car.

Clay goes to Blair's father's party. Clay calls Blair to see if she knows where Julian is, but she is mad at him. Clay goes to a party at Kim's house. Clay and Rip go to a restaurant named Pages. In the bathroom, Clay sees graffiti that says, "Julian gives great head. And is dead." Clay remembers being in Palm Springs and walking around at night when it was very spooky. Clay goes to a party in a garage downtown. Dimitri is drunk and he hurts himself by punching his hand through a window.

Clay watches more religious television and takes some cocaine before his date with Blair. A phrase from the religious television show resonates in his mind: "Let this be a night of Deliverance." Blair drinks too much liquor and then hits a coyote while she's driving. She cries while Clay watches it die. Then they go home and have sex.

The next night, Blair and Clay go to Kim's party. They go outside and have sex. Clay and his father go to a restaurant in Hollywood called Trumps. His father has started wearing a cowboy hat and tells Clay to heed the advice of astrology.

### Commentary

Clay's visit to the house of a man named Dead is a metaphorical visit to Death itself, or himself. The drugs and perverse sexual climate at Dead's house represent the connection between this decadent way of living and death.

While at the party in the parking garage, Clay looks out the window and sees a huge cathedral with a cross on top pointed toward the moon. Though the meaning is not clear, the presence of the metaphor is intentional. The other religious imagery in this section is the television evangelist's phrase that resonates in Clay's mind: "Let this be a night of Deliverance." Clay's frequent viewing of religious television indicates that he is searching for a deeper meaning in life. Unfortunately, in the 1980s, religion has become devalued, because it is on television.

When Blair accidentally kills a coyote by running over it with her car, we see how mankind (as represented by a drunk, young, rich teenager in a sports car) is foolishly tampering with the natural order of things (a jaywalking coyote).

# LXXII–LXXXIV

### Summary

Clay goes to Daniel's house, then to Kim's house, where Muriel is screaming. Clay and Rip go to a record company, where Rip sells cocaine to a young executive. No one will tell Clay where Julian is. Clay and Trent go to a party. In one of the rooms, ten young boys are watching a "snuff" movie, in which a large black man with an erection has sex with a boy and a girl before sticking nails and an ice pick into the girl's neck. After a while, Clay leaves the room. Eventually Trent comes out with an erection. Clay remembers his grandmother sitting quietly in Palm Springs.

Trent and Clay take some cocaine in a hamburger restaurant. Clay's nose hurts and starts bleeding. Clay remembers being in Palm Springs when his grandmother started coughing up blood because she was dying of pancreatic cancer. Alana visits Clay at home. She cries, talks about her recent abortion and falls asleep. After she leaves, Clay flushes his toilet and it is filled with Alana's blood.

Clay goes to Daniel's house to smoke marijuana. Daniel talks about a young girl he knows whose drug dealer gives her lots of drugs and takes her to parties where everybody has sex with her. Daniel says that he's not going back to school and that he's going to write a screenplay instead. Clay calls his psychoanalyst and says he is discontinuing his treatment.

Clay remembers flying out of Palm Springs after his grandmother died.

He has fond memories of her. Clay goes to his old elementary school, which now looks different. This makes him sad.

## Commentary

In this segment of the book, the events depicted get more and more horrifying. The "snuff" movie shows that Clay's peers condone murder and rape of other people as a form of entertainment. This bears comparison to Roman orgies and gladiator fights, and to what eventually happened to the Roman Empire. The theme of death—as symbolized by a dead coyote, a "snuff" movie, Clay's dead grandmother and the man named Dead—pervades the book. So omnipresent is this theme that when *Less Than Zero* was made into a movie, the character Julian literally died at the end.

In the Palm Springs flashback segments, we learn why we must pity Clay, rather than scorn or laugh at him. His grandmother died, and because he liked her this tragic incident has cast a shadow over the rest of his life.

# LXXXV–XCIII

## Summary

Clay meets Julian, who says he can pay Clay back. They go to Finn's apartment. Finn employs Julian to have sex with men for money. He thinks Clay has come for similar work. Julian starts crying. Julian says he is finished with drugs and does not want to be a male prostitute anymore. Finn gives Julian an injection of drugs, and he changes his mind.

Clay and Julian go to a hotel, where they meet a Midwestern businessman. He tells Julian to undress and for Clay to sit in a chair and watch. Clay goes into the bathroom and tries to vomit. When he comes back out, the man rolls Julian over and begins having sex with him. Clay watches for five hours, and then he and Julian leave.

Clay, Julian and Finn go to a party in Bel Air, an exclusive and wealthy part of Los Angeles. Clay goes into the bathroom and takes some cocaine. Finn and Julian come in. Finn pushes Julian. Clay does nothing. Julian says Finn has turned him into a whore, but Finn maintains that Julian did this to himself. Finn gives Julian an injection and then leads him into a room where people are having sex. Clay runs away.

Clay meets Trent and Rip at a nightclub called The Roxy. Ross takes them all to see a dead body in an alleyway. Then they all go to Rip's house, where there is a delirious, naked 12-year-old girl tied to the bed. Spin gives her an injection of drugs and then takes off his clothes and starts to have sex with her in her mouth. Clay and Rip leave the room, even though Spin said it was okay if they watched. Clay says what Spin is doing is wrong, but Rip maintains that if one wants something, one has the right to take it. Clay leaves in a huff.

Clay remembers reading about a wild party at which a girl was raped repeatedly, strangled and finally had her throat slit and her breasts lopped off and replaced with candles. Then her body was deposited on a swing set. Clay drives out toward the desert and thinks about the time he used to spend in Palm Springs.

## Commentary

In a 1986 interview, Ellis said, "All the themes of the book come together in [the 12-year-old girl rape] scene. There is a bit of dialogue between the two characters—if you're reading so far and you don't get what the book is about, that is the scene where most people go 'Aha. I see what this guy's about. Yeah . . . !' "

Clay, like Shakespeare's adolescent character Hamlet, is paralyzed by hesitation. Instead of intervening during the rape, Clay leaves the room. But he is not totally apathetic; he *does* feel that these actions are bad, and in the crucial conversation he articulates this: "It's . . . It's . . . I don't think it's right." Rip responds "If you want to do something, you have the right to do it." Clay and Rip's uncharacteristically emotional and articulate conversation contains the entire meaning of the novel: many of the wealthy young people in Los Angeles are self-centered and amoral, but some retain a few qualms about self-indulgent, debasing behavior.

# XCIV–CVIII

## Summary

Clay spends the week before he leaves for school watching television. He tells Alana that he did not have a good time in Los Angeles. Clay meets Finn in a supermarket and they say hello to each other. He also hears that Julian has been beaten up.

Clay has lunch with Blair at The Old World restaurant, a screenwriter hangout in Hollywood. Blair asks Clay if he ever loved her. Clay hems and haws. Blair says that she loved him, but he was "never there." Clay says, "Nothing makes me happy. I like nothing. . . . I don't want to care. If I care about things, it'll just be worse, it'll just be another thing to worry about. It's less painful if I don't care."

Blair calls Clay and asks him not to leave. He says he will return. Clay drives around alone, thinking. His final thought is about images brought to his mind by a song called "Los Angeles" by a pop combo named X. The images include people going crazy because they live in the city, ambitious parents eating their own children, and teenagers being blinded by the sun—"Images so violent and malicious that they seemed to be my only point of reference for a long time afterwards. After I left."

## Commentary

Clay's conversation with Blair reveals the reason for his detachment and aloofness. He is trying to avoid the pain that accompanies caring about others, or "merging." Also, like Shakespeare's character King Lear, Clay uses the word "nothing" repeatedly in his short monologue. This recurring theme of nothingness bolsters Ellis's argument that spiritual, intellectual and emotional emptiness make Los Angeles a decadent place.

Clay's final thoughts on Los Angeles accurately and succinctly summarize the point of the whole novel. Los Angeles is a bad city, prone to excess and decadence. It's no place to raise a child, and the children who are raised there become emotionally, intellectually and spiritually scarred for life, and they consequently behave badly.

## QUESTIONS FOR REVIEW

1. Ellis has said, ''Morality is definitely your own code of ethics day by day expressing individualism. I believe in individuality. If I have a moral code of ethics that I think people should have, individuality would top it off.'' What does this mean?

2. The critic Eliot Fremont-Smith has called *Less Than Zero* ''a killer— sexy, sassy, and sad. . . . It's a teenage slice-of-death novel, no holds barred.'' Do you agree? Explain. How much older than 50 do you think Fremont-Smith is?

3. What effect did Ellis hope to achieve by italicizing certain passages in the book? Do you care?

# BIOGRAPHICAL NOTE

Jill Eisenstadt was born in 1963 in Far Rockaway, New York. She attended Bennington, an exclusive, progressive, expensive arts-oriented college in Vermont, where she was a contemporary of Bret Easton Ellis's. She studied fiction writing under best-selling non-fiction author Joe McGinnis, who discovered Ellis. At Bennington, she met Ellis when she overheard him calling one of her short stories ''the silliest garbage I've ever seen.'' She studied fiction writing in the Columbia University writing program and worked in advertising. Eventually, Ellis circulated her novel *From Rockaway* among his publishing acquaintances in New York, and Joe McGinnis introduced her to the agent Morton Janklow. *From Rockaway* was published by Alfred A. Knopf in 1987, when Eisenstadt was 24. She is currently writing a book about ''twin brothers whose father runs a beauty parlor.''

# *From Rockaway* by Jill Eisenstadt

## LIST OF CHARACTERS

*Alex*

A young woman from Far Rockaway, a working-class suburb of New York, who goes to Camden, an exclusive college in New Hampshire.

*Timmy*

Alex's former boyfriend who stays behind in Far Rockaway, working as a lifeguard. His father left his mother.

36

### Chowderhead
Another member of Alex and Timmy's social circle, who also works as a lifeguard.

### Peg
A fourth member of the social circle, who goes to a junior college and then drops out.

### Joe
An eccentric Camden student whom Alex likes.

### Sloane
A working-class teenage ne'er-do-well from Rockaway.

# PROLOGUE; 1

### Summary
Tim, Peg, Alex and Chowderhead ride around in a limousine after their high school prom, drinking liquor and smoking marijuana. Alex considers having sex with Timmy, but she thinks she is beginning to menstruate. They all go to the beach where they meet Seaver, a homeless person without a tongue who is confined to a wheelchair. They build a bonfire. When Peg and Alex go off from the group to urinate, they discover that Alex is not getting her period after all, but that Peg is. Alex and Timmy go to the lifeguard shack. Timmy takes off his clothes, but Alex starts to feel sick. She goes home.

Later in the summer, Timmy's mother is angry with him, due to his reprobate behavior and marijuana-smoking lifestyle. Timmy and his mother moved to Rockaway when Timmy's father's fingers were chopped off by a lawn mower. He subsequently fell in love with the lady who helped him rehabilitate his reattached fingers.

### Commentary
The conflict between social classes is a main theme of *From Rockaway*. The novel also examines the difficulties of leaving home for the first time and making new friends. But the novel is not *only* about intellectual topics; in a way, it also tells a story.

Like most of the novels in this genre, *From Rockaway* is autobiographical, and, like Bret Easton Ellis's *Rules of Attraction*, it is about Bennington College (which Eisenstadt and Ellis both call "Camden"). The novel thus serves an historical function: Eisenstadt preserves for history a description of life at a particular New Hampshire college in the 1980s. Ellis's *The Rules of Attraction* performs the same function, but we must remember that the two novels are not redundant or unnecessary. After all, Bennington College might eventually be of interest to scholars; much like Bloomsbury at the turn of the century and Paris in the 1920s, Bennington in the 1980s produced at least two famous young novelists.

## 2–4

### Summary

On lifeguard duty, Chowderhead meets a spunky little boy who is lost, and takes him home. Chowderhead's father yells at Chowderhead because Chowderhead doesn't know who the boy is. Chowderhead and the boy escape on a bicycle and go to the rich people's section of town.

The police yell at Chowderhead, but the little boy persuades them that Chowderhead is innocent.

Later, Timmy starts to write a letter to Alex but gives up. Sloane fools Timmy into thinking someone is drowning, and Timmy falls for the trick. Later in the summer, Alex and Timmy exchange letters. Eventually, Alex stops writing.

### Commentary

Chowderhead, as his name suggests, is lonely, misunderstood and dim-witted. The trip to the wealthy part of town is lush with imagery that highlights the rigid stratification of social classes—even in Long Island, a supposedly pluralistic society.

We understand that Sloane is less smart than Timmy, because he dropped out of high school and speaks primarily in partial words without apostrophes.

## 5–7

### Summary

Alex and a character named "Roommate" are in their dorm room at Camden College. Roommate sleeps with makeup on in case Lars, the person she has sex with, comes over. Alex likes a fellow named Joe. Everyone thinks Alex and Joe have sex together, but they don't really. Alex, however, listens to Roommate and Lars having sex.

When Alex is at her job sweeping up the Pub, Joe comes to see her, but he leaves with June. Later, Joe tells Alex she is too nice. Alex and her friend Ponzio go to the Pub and get drunk. Joe has left with June again.

Before Christmas break, Alex looks at a list that she and Roommate have made of all the fellows they've had sex with. Joe drives down to Rockaway with Alex. Alex looks at her old bedroom, which has changed. This makes her sad.

### Commentary

Eisenstadt's writing is similar to that of Marcel Proust: she creates a rich fictional world by accumulating sharp observations and rendering them in fresh, descriptive language. For instance, she notes that college cafeteria food often seems unpalatable, that college roommates often do not get along, that men think women take too long in the bathroom and that drinking liquor often makes one feel tired and ill the following day.

The permissive sexual atmosphere on campus in the late 1980s recalls the days of "hippie free love" in the late 1960s. Exclusive colleges in the late

38

1960s also produced many, many prodigious young writers whose contributions to American fiction have endured to this day.

## 8–10

*Summary*
    The movie theater in Rockaway catches fire while Chowderhead's mother is watching a martial-arts movie. Timmy and Chowderhead go to the burned-out theater, where they see Seaver inside, eating candy. Later, Timmy, Peg, Chowderhead and a Jewish boy get in a fight, insulting each other's respective Irish and Jewish ethnic backgrounds. Timmy tries to intercede, but later he beats up a random straggler from the other group.
    Peg goes to visit Alex at Camden. Alex, while urinating, recalls how she and Peg used to urinate together on the beach in Rockaway. They smoke marijuana. Peg thinks Camden has too many unpleasant, rich students. They go to the "Dress to Get Laid" party. Peg gets in a fight with the girlfriend of a guy who urinated on her and then called her a "dyke," a colloquialism for lesbian. Alex and Ponzio make Peg go outside and smoke some more marijuana.

*Commentary*
    The social "friction" between two ethnic groups causes an emotional "heat" so intense that Timmy figuratively "explodes" in a violent rage. Eisenstadt's examination of social and ethnic tensions recalls the works of Ralph Ellison, George Orwell and Norman Lear.
    Those who have read Ellis's *The Rules of Attraction* or attended Bennington College will recognize the "Dressed to [Have Sex]" party and many other shared details. In *The Rules of Attraction*, Ellis writes of "cute Joseph who Alex-nice-girl-from-Rockaway is sleeping with" and Alex's "awful roommate." While this may seem self-indulgent or even "cutesy," we must remember that even a novelist's imagination has its limits; at a certain point, the novelist must draw on the only things he or she knows well. In this case, that would be Bennington College and the works of other young novelists in the same genre.

## 11–12

*Summary*
    In the summer, Chowder and Timmy are going to bartenders' school. Timmy has an extra ticket to a cruise called "Cruise to Nowhere." He invites Peg. Chowder takes Alicia. Timmy wins $500 playing roulette.
    Later in the summer, Alex is on the boardwalk when the sandbar at the beach breaks. Many people are thrown into deep water. All the lifeguards try to save people. Timmy is the only lifeguard who fails and allows a swimmer to die.

*Commentary*

The "Cruise to Nowhere" is a metaphor for life in Rockaway, as Timmy and his friends see it: while they keep moving, they essentially are going "nowhere." As in the play *No Exit* by Jean-Paul Sartre, there is no exit.

The broken sandbar is a climactic scene, rich with metaphorical implications. Timmy learns that even though love conquers all, life is full of surprises, and if something can go wrong, it will. The scope of the disaster shows that it never rains, it pours, but that ultimately every cloud has a silver lining: even though Timmy has forgotten to expect the unexpected and literally look before he leaps, the ordeal gives him grace to accept with serenity the things that cannot be changed, courage to change the things which should be changed and the wisdom to tell the one from the other.

# 13–14; EPILOGUE

*Summary*

The lifeguards take Timmy to the ritual "Death Keg" party they have every time a swimmer dies. They toss him in the air and drink liquor. Chowder urinates and imagines a stream of urine powerful enough to douse the nearby lighthouse. They bury Timmy up to the neck in the sand near the campfire. Alex kisses him. Eventually, the lifeguards dunk him in the water and he breaks free, considering suicide, but then they pull him from the water.

They all go to the bridge for their ritual dangerous jump. Chowderhead tries to persuade Timmy not to participate in the bridge jump. Sloane throws his dog off the bridge because it barks too much. Timmy decides not to jump, realizing that this is how Seaver became a crippled mute. Sloane moans over the dead dog. His father is in an alcohol-abuse rehabilitation program, his mother is dead and now he has killed his dog.

In the Epilogue, Timmy writes a letter to his estranged father, saying he has adopted Seaver. He tells his father that his feelings for Alex are like his mother's feelings for God.

*Commentary*

The discovery that Seaver was crippled by jumping off the bridge leads Timmy to reject the self-destructive traditions of Rockaway. We realize that Timmy and his friends have also created a metaphorical religion of their own: not a religion of churches and irrelevant traditions, but a religion of the beach and the boardwalk, with brand-new traditions that are more meaningful to today's young people.

# QUESTION FOR REVIEW

1. Discuss the theme of urination in *From Rockaway*, making reference to at least three of the following: Alex and Peg urinating back-to-back

on the beach, a drunken party-goer urinating on Peg, Alex fondly recalling the days when she and Peg used to urinate together on the beach, Chowderhead's assessment that women spend too much time urinating and Chowderhead's desire to urinate far enough and forcefully enough to douse a nearby lighthouse.

## SUGGESTION FOR FURTHER READING

"About Last Night" (*Interview*, October 1987): Eisenstadt and Bret Easton Ellis interview each other.

# *The Rules of Attraction* by Bret Easton Ellis

## LIST OF CHARACTERS

*Lauren*
A student at Camden, an exclusive college in New Hampshire.

*Sean*
A student at Camden, an exclusive college in New Hampshire.

*Paul*
A student at Camden, an exclusive college in New Hampshire.

# I

### Summary
At a party, Lauren gets very drunk and lures a student from New York University to a friend's dorm room by claiming she has some marijuana. She passes out, and when she wakes up someone is having sex with her. She soon realizes that a second person is having sex with her also. Meanwhile, someone else is vomiting on the floor.

In the morning, Lauren discovers both the NYU student and a naked "townie" in the room, but she is not sure which one she lost her virginity to. The naked "townie" tells her an off-color joke about an elephant and a mouse having sex.

### Commentary
Readers inclined to take a prurient interest in *The Rules of Attraction* should be warned that the shocking sex scene in the prologue is uncharacteristic of the rest of the novel. While there are numerous incidents of a sexual nature in the book, the author avoids gratuitous titillation by employing a "tell—

don't show'' prose style. Most sexual activity is described in a flat, decidedly nonsensual manner that omits almost all details and description (the only exceptions being the slightly more detailed passages on pages 83, 114–15 and 167 of the paperback edition). One of the author's chief goals is to deglamorize drug abuse, the pleasures of youth, and sex. He does this by making even the most shocking and exciting topics seem mundane and even tedious. Those in search of light reading should know that *The Rules of Attraction* is a serious work, the intention of which is not to entertain or amuse.

# II–VII

### Summary

Three years later, Sean goes to Deirdre's dorm room even though she is drunk and overweight. She has trouble inserting her diaphragm. Sean tries unsuccessfully to have sex with her and then leaves. At the same party, Paul goes home with a drunk freshman named Katrina, but when she passes out, he decides not to have sex with her. Lauren has sex with a freshman named Steve even though she misses her boyfriend Victor, who is in Europe.

Meanwhile, Victor travels in Europe, looking for a girl from Camden named Jaime. He uses a variety of drugs and has sex with men and women of various nationalities. Paul remembers dating Mitchell in New York during summer vacation. They would see plays, go to bars and have sex. Sean has sex with Deirdre and then drives his motorcycle into town to buy drugs. Later, he tries to get some money from Marc, who is injecting heroin at the time.

### Commentary

*The Rules of Attraction*, like Melville's *Moby-Dick* and Nabokov's *Lolita*, was widely misunderstood when it was first published. Many people thought it was just a poorly written adolescent hodgepodge that relied on a methodical cataloging of sexual acts and drug intake in lieu of any narrative structure, plausible characters, fresh observations or readable prose. The novel must be reassessed.

Like John Barth and William Gaddis, Bret Easton Ellis writes ''difficult'' fiction. The story is told not through a linear or easily comprehensible plot, but rather through short passages of first-person narration by 14 different characters. The characters are just faceless names, and descriptions of setting are nonexistent. This may seem confusing or intimidating at first, but we must remember that Ellis's approach to fiction is experimental. Once we're accustomed to this new style, we see how the novel's fractured, kaleidoscopic narration more accurately reflects the confusion of contemporary life at an exclusive New England college in the late 1980s.

This ''difficult'' fiction forces the reader to pay very close attention to the novel in order to figure out what's happening in it. The reader who reads this book without expending the intellectual energy necessary to glean order from its chaos will probably not find much in it at all.

# VIII–X

## Summary

At breakfast, Paul sits with three homosexual fellows who have been taking the drug crystal Methedrine all night. Lauren has breakfast with friends, who are discussing Sara's pregnancy and imminent abortion. Lauren remembers she too has had sex with Tim, the person who made Sara pregnant. Steve, with whom Lauren had sex the night before, comes to talk to her, and she tries to ignore him. She takes a bath, smokes some marijuana and thinks about Victor.

Sean longs for Candice, even though she is having sex with Mitchell. Sean wonders who has been leaving notes in his mailbox. At lunch Sean and his friends joke about Sara's abortion. Sean remembers he had sex with Sara a few times, but he can't remember whether she performs great fellatio or has the intrauterine birth control device that he almost hurt his penis on once. Deirdre, whom Sean has had sex with, comes to the table and he tries to ignore her.

## Commentary

In this section, as in every section of the book, we are overwhelmed by the amount of casual sexual activity and drug abuse that occurs on this campus. At Camden the sexual act has become devalued—a perceptive, telling metaphor for the devaluation of sex in general in the 1980s. Sean remembers that he has had sex with Sara, but he can't remember whether the sexual act was good (well-performed fellatio) or bad (dangerously sharp IUD).

By now the reader has probably noticed that the novel sounds very much like the diary of a college student. Indeed, Ellis's literary reputation is based primarily on the autobiographical nature of his work. Why should we care about Ellis's life? Because *The Rules of Attraction* captures and chronicles the minutiae of contemporary life in a particular time and place (an exclusive New England college in the late 1980s)—just as F. Scott Fitzgerald immortalized the Jazz Age in *The Great Gatsby* and Norman Mailer captured the horrors of World War II in *The Naked and the Dead*.

# XI–XVI

## Summary

At a party, Paul talks to Mitchell. Paul has had sex with Mitchell, but Mitchell doesn't like Paul to talk to him in public or just after he has ejaculated. Paul thinks about pushing Candice down an embankment because she is with Mitchell. Meanwhile, Sean watches Candice, with whom he wants to have sex. Sean asks Roxanne if she would like to have sex with him, and when she declines he goes back to his room, breaks some things and then returns to the party.

Lauren and her friend Judy are in Lauren's art studio drinking liquor and smoking marijuana. Lauren has had an argument with her mother on the phone.

Lauren's divorced father's girlfriend is only 25 years old. Lauren and Judy go to the campus pub and smoke marijuana.

Paul and Sean meet at the party. Paul hears Sean incorrectly and thinks Sean is inviting him out for foreign food the next night, when actually Sean is just asking him to buy a case of beer. Sean decides to go anyway. Sean has sex with Deirdre again.

## Commentary

In this section we learn that Lauren's parents are divorced and that her father dates young women. A traumatic childhood is a hallmark of this literary canon. The bad behavior and petulant personalities of the main characters in these books would render them unsympathetic to most readers if we weren't told that bad things had happened to them in the past and affected them permanently. Thus it comes as no surprise when we later learn that Paul's parents are getting divorced and that Sean's father is terminally ill and his mother insane.

## XVII–XXVII

### Summary

Mary, who has been secretly leaving love notes for Sean, longs to take him home to Arizona. Paul has been whispering Sean's name to himself all day, at one point with a pillow between his legs. While Paul is preparing for his date with Sean, Raymond enters and says that Harry has tried to commit suicide because he discovered he was adopted. Paul goes to Harry's room and then they drive Harry to the hospital. The doctor insists, despite Harry's protestations, that Harry is dead, so they leave the hospital.

Sean finds another note in his mailbox. He sees Dan, who had been having sex with Candice the term before. Sean runs into Paul at a party. Some bad people from Dartmouth, an actual exclusive college in New Hampshire, have come to the party uninvited, thinking it's the "Dressed to Get Screwed" party. Paul secretly wants to have sex with them. Sean and Paul go to Paul's room.

Lauren has sex with Judy's boyfriend Franklin. In Paul's room, Sean smokes marijuana. Paul and Sean neck and then masturbate each other. Sean's roommate Bertrand wants to have sex with Lauren, but his girlfriend Beba doesn't know it.

### Commentary

Bertrand's monologue about his secret desire to have sex with Lauren is a tour de force of erudite, cosmopolitan writing because it is in French. Though most of the novel is written in a conversational tone in English, Ellis is not afraid to challenge the reader by employing his knowledge of French. Also, because Bertrand is French, it is more true-to-life that he thinks in French.

The scene in the hospital is a tour de force of *confusing black humor*. As with Joseph Heller's *Catch-22*, the reader is unsure whether the action is meant to be funny or horrifying, and the author provides few clues. It's probably supposed to be funny, though.

44

# XXVIII–XXXVII

### Summary

Sean and Paul spend a lot of time together, having sex. Sean likes to shoplift, and Paul likes Sean's body and riding on Sean's motorcycle. Stuart longs to have sex with Paul, even though Stuart's roommate Dennis wants to have sex with Stuart. Sean remembers a "hippie" girl he had sex with freshman year. The "hippie" girl thought that everyone and everything was beautiful. This infuriated Sean, but he had sex with her anyway, before breaking up with her and having sex with her best friend.

Sean takes cough syrup with codeine to get "high." Paul finds the notes someone leaves for Sean, but like Sean, he doesn't know who's sending them. Lately Lauren has been having sex with Franklin, and Judy has been having sex with the freshman named Steve. Lauren still misses Victor. Paul's mother phones to say her Cadillac has been stolen and that she is flying to Boston from Chicago and wants Paul to meet her. Mary, the secret note writer, still longs for Sean.

Paul wants Sean to go to Boston with him, but Sean doesn't want to go. Sean sits in the Pub with Paul, while people discuss Tony's steel sculpture of a vagina. Someone says that a pretty girl has had sex with Lauren. Sean finds Susan, who says she has a boyfriend, but she performs fellatio on Sean anyway. Then he has sex with her, and she starts to cry. Although Lauren is spending more time with Franklin, his interest in science fiction and astrology annoys her.

### Commentary

In this section, Ellis expands on the theme of romantic obsession. Mary longs for Sean from afar and leaves anonymous notes for him, but he doesn't even know she exists until she kills herself later in the book. Stuart's burning desire to have sex with Paul is ultimately fruitless. We feel the pain of these minor characters; they too have sexual and romantic desires, but unlike the main characters in the book, they never get to have sex with any of the other main characters in the book.

# XXXVIII–LI

### Summary

Sean takes a lot of cough syrup and dreams about Lauren. Paul rides the bus to Boston. He wants to have sex with a boy who looks like Sean. The students in the back of the bus smoke marijuana. Sean tries to talk to Lauren at lunch, because he thinks she's been leaving the notes for him. Lauren is standing next to Judy, who dislikes Sean because she once had sex with him.

Mary is sad because Sean doesn't notice her and because her father dates young women. Paul checks into his mother's hotel in Boston and wonders if he'll have sex with his boyhood friend Richard Jared, who's coming to Boston with his mother and Sean's mother. Lauren tells Franklin she's leaving him. Then they have sex.

After smoking some marijuana, Stuart thinks about asking Paul over to his hair-dyeing party even though he, Stuart, has been having sex with Dennis. Paul thinks his mother has been dating her psychologist. He worries about who Sean will have sex with while he's gone. Paul's mother and her friend Mrs. Jared share a Seconal sedative pill. When Richard arrives, he is wearing punk-rock clothing and drinking from a bottle of liquor. He insists on being called "Dick."

### Commentary

Paul's annoyance with the young students on the bus provides great insight into the source of his (and Sean's and Lauren's) discontent. They are members of a particular generation that is slowly being supplanted by a younger generation with different habits and even shallower values. Sean, Paul and Lauren notice sadly that this younger generation does not drink as much and that many of them are politically conservative. Ellis is acutely aware that he is chronicling the decline of a particular "golden age" of undergraduate life.

Ellis's as-yet-unnamed generation will probably go down in history as the 1980s equivalent of the "Lost Generation" of the 1920s: *The Rules of Attraction* alone contains more sexual activity and drunkenness than all the novels of Fitzgerald and Hemingway combined. Just as the horrors of World War I disillusioned and embittered a whole generation of American youth in the 1920s, so does the divorce or premature death of one's parents traumatize almost every single character in this 1980s literary canon.

# LII–LVI

### Summary

Sean gets drunk and masturbates while thinking about Lauren. He wonders what her sexual habits are and decides he won't go to bed with a girl who won't let him ejaculate into her mouth. Lauren and Judy smoke marijuana and make a list of all the people they've had sex with. Sean goes to Rupert's room, where Rupert is taking cocaine. Rupert gives Sean drugs to sell to freshmen at the upcoming party. Rupert's Brazilian assistant is having sex with Roxanne.

At the annual "Dressed to Get Screwed" party, Reggie bluntly asks Lauren to perform fellatio on him. She declines. Tim and Tony urinate into a beer bottle and give it to Deirdre. Lauren calls Victor (who is now in New York) from a phone booth. Jaime answers the phone, so Lauren hangs up. Sean tries to make Lauren interested in him. Then he grabs her, and they go outside. Stuart takes some cocaine and goes to the party, hoping to be noticed by Paul. He does a crazy dance in his underwear. Everyone watches and applauds. Mary watches Sean leave with Lauren and then goes to an embankment and contemplates suicide.

Meanwhile in Boston, Paul, Richard and their mothers have drinks in the hotel bar. Richard behaves rudely, tells an off-color joke and then leaves.

46

Paul's mother tells him that she's divorcing his father and that they've lived apart since he went to college.

## Commentary

Sean desires an intimacy with Lauren that goes far beyond mere sexual contact. He thinks that he would not want to go out with her if she won't let him ejaculate inside her mouth—surely one of the most intimate of all possible sexual acts. Lauren too longs for intimacy: even though she has already had sex with six men in this story, she bluntly refuses to perform fellatio on Reggie. The requested act is too intimate; despite her nihilism and promiscuity, Lauren seems to reserve some romantic hope that the right person will eventually come along, a "Mr. Right" whom she will feel comfortable performing fellatio on.

# LVII–LXVI

## Summary

Lauren and Sean go to the apartment of two lesbians, where they engage in droll banter. Then they go to Sean's room. Lauren misses Victor, but she has sex with Sean anyway. The sexual act is unfulfilling for Sean because he is sober and because Lauren is experiencing vaginal lubrication problems. In Boston, Paul and Richard argue about their childhood, and then they have sex.

Mary commits suicide by slitting her wrists in the bathtub. While Sean is asleep, Lauren remembers her relationship with Paul and wonders what went wrong with it. On the bus ride back to school, Paul tries to masturbate in the bathroom. After a night of taking the drug Ecstasy and having sex with Tim and Norris, Roxanne finds Mary dead in the bathtub. Rupert gives Roxanne the drug Xanax. Paul sees Lauren looking out of Sean's window and knows that they have been having sex.

## Commentary

Mary's suicide depicts the incredible pain of adolescence, which often continues on into one's college years. Also in this section, we see that the web of relationships in the novel forms a classic *love triangle* (see diagram on page 47). Sean, Paul and Lauren have each had sex with each other. Ellis's version of the love triangle is far more ambitious than most writers attempt, due to the fact that it involves at least 37 different characters.

# LXVII–LXXII

## Summary

Sean and Lauren smoke marijuana with Judy and her new lover, Frank. Sean and Lauren have sex while Judy and Frank listen. Clay longs for his home in California. He has recently had sex with "some rich boys, with some richer girls, a couple from Northern California, a French teacher, a girl from Vassar [an actual exclusive college in New York State] who knows one of my sisters, some girl who couldn't stop drinking Nyquil" and others.

Sean tells Paul he has spoiled their relationship by introducing sex. Sean

# THE *RULES OF ATTRACTION* LOVE TRIANGLE

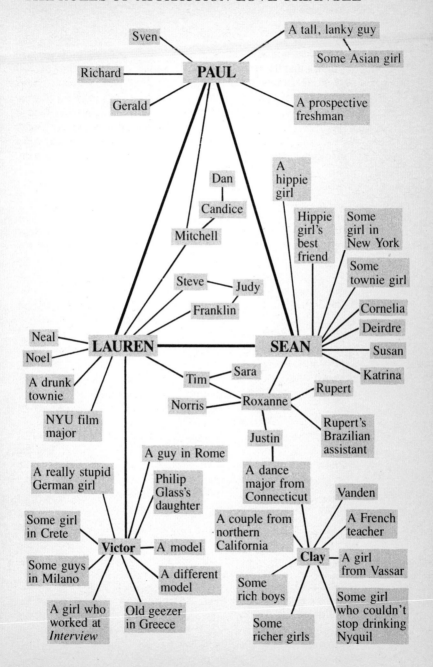

48

is overcome with desire for Lauren, even though he doesn't like her poetry about masturbation. He says he spends hours and hours performing cunnilingus on her. Lauren thinks sex with Sean is merely passable and that having cunnilingus performed on her for hours and hours is not her idea of a good time. They take the drug Ecstasy together.

Lauren takes Sean to a get-together at the house of an elderly Italian poetry professor. The students there drink liquor and discuss poetry, art and punk rock music in a pretentious way. One of them, Stump, is working on a long poem about people having sex with dogs. After taking some of the prescription drug Librium from the professor's medicine cabinet, Sean passes out. Later he wants to leave, but Lauren wants to stay because the elderly professor has fallen down. Sean leaves, meets Judy at the campus pub and has sex with her.

### Commentary

As Sean and Lauren's relationship grows more intimate, we discover that there are limits to how well an individual can know another person. As Lauren tells Sean in a later section, "No one ever *knows* anyone." Ellis uses a sexual metaphor to illuminate this philosophical concept. Sean thinks that Lauren likes him because he performs cunnilingus on her for hours and hours on end. Lauren doesn't actually enjoy this, but she doesn't want to hurt Sean's feelings by telling him to stop. Thus, because neither is capable of speaking intimately with the other, Sean and Lauren seem stuck on a perpetual treadmill, engaged in a mutually disagreeable act that has no forseeable end.

Clay, the narrator of Ellis's first novel, *Less Than Zero*, makes a "cameo appearance" in this section. Clay's observation that "People are afraid to merge on campus" brilliantly echoes the famous opening of *Less Than Zero* ("People are afraid to merge on freeways in Los Angeles"). Clay's reappearance shows that he is a mildly fictionalized version of the author himself—much like Tama Janowitz's Eleanor character, Jill Eisenstadt's Alex, Lisa Pliscou's Miranda, Peter Farrelly's Tim, Mark Lindquist's Zeke, Lisa Grunwald's Jen, Susan Minot's Sophie and Jay McInerney's Jamie.

# LXXIII–LXXX

### Summary

Lauren confronts Sean with the fact that he had sex with Judy, but he denies it, unaware that Judy herself told Lauren. Paul has sex with a prospective freshman boy. Sean tries to masturbate, but he gets depressed because the *Playboy* magazine centerfold model is two years younger than he. Partly because of this, he tries to hang himself using a tie, but the tie breaks.

Sean and Norris go shopping. Norris picks up his prescription for the drug Ritalin, and Sean buys a tube of fake blood. Sean goes to a class and fantasizes about having sex with a girl who's there. Sean's counselor tells him he's failing four classes. Sean tries to overdose on the cold medication Actifed, but Norris wakes him up. In the shower Sean tries to slash his wrists, but the razor is too dull. After he sees Lauren with Justin at a party, Sean breaks a pumpkin on her door and leaves her a nasty note. He goes back to his room and puts the fake blood all over himself. Lauren comes in and is angered by his macabre prank. Then she kisses him.

Lauren tells Sean she likes someone else. When Lauren sees Paul staring at Sean, she remembers that Paul had sex with Mitchell. Roxanne and Justin are having sex. Victor returns to school and smokes marijuana with Rupert. Susie tries unsuccessfully to kill herself. Bertrand tells Lauren that he loves her, in French.

## Commentary

Sean asks Lauren, "Since, like, when does having sex with someone else mean, like, I'm not faithful to you?" Sean obviously believes in a type of romantic fidelity that goes beyond sexual fidelity. But what is this fidelity based on? It's a thorny question, and it is obviously one that the main characters are probably wrestling with in their own minds.

Sean's purchase of fake blood foreshadows the macabre fake suicide that occurs only a few pages later. This is an example of Ellis's unorthodox use of plot. Rather than surprising the reader with unexpected events, Ellis's plots deliberately fulfill our expectations. Ellis wants the readers themselves to feel more deeply the same dilemma that the characters in the novel are trying constantly to resolve: Why go on when one knows that the future holds no surprises?

# LXXXI–LXXXVIII

## Summary

Sean goes to New York because his father is dying from a terminal illness. His mother has already been committed to an asylum. Sean behaves rudely at the hospital. Sean's brother Patrick doesn't understand Sean's bad attitude. Their father is very rich, but Sean doesn't want to join his firm. Sean and Robert take cocaine in a bathroom and then pick up some girls and go to a nightclub discothéque named Palladium. They have both had sex with Cornelia at some time in the past, perhaps simultaneously. Sean returns to Camden.

Paul notices that a fellow he once had sex with is now having sex with an Asian girl. Lauren, who once had sex with Neal, takes a dosage of the hallucinogen LSD with Noel. She has a urinary tract infection, but she has sex with Noel anyway. Sean longs for Lauren and promises himself that he will forgo one-night stands in the future. Gerald tries to masturbate Paul while they drive in Lizzie's car. Later, Paul has sex with Gerald even though he wanted to have sex with a Korean fellow who was taking LSD. After that, Sean and Paul go out in the woods and have sex in the snow.

## Commentary

By this point in the novel, Ellis has achieved his goal of deglamorizing sex, drugs and other collegiate activities. Why, then, should one continue reading? Ellis himself has answered this question in his first book, *Less Than*

*Zero*: in that novel Clay accompanies Julian to his job as a homosexual prostitute because he wants "to see the worst." Like Clay, we must continue reading because we want "to see the worst."

Ellis tests our commitment to the fiction process by creating a tableau of characters so hollow that he is almost daring us to put the book down. He thus reaffirms that fiction is a process that requires the reader to make as much of a commitment as the author has. Ellis knows it would be rude for his readers not to take the time to finish reading a novel that he has taken the time to finish writing.

# LXXXIX–XCVI

### Summary

Lauren tells Sean that she's pregnant. He proposes marriage to her. She thinks the person who got her pregnant is either Sean, Franklin, Noel, Steve or Paul. Sean and Lauren visit married friends in New York City. They both grow dissatisfied with the prospect of married life after watching their materialistic New York friends consider buying a foreign car. Paul takes hallucinogenic mushrooms with Gerald. At a party Paul talks to Victor, with whom he wants to have sex.

Lauren and Sean drive around smoking marijuana and taking cocaine but not speaking to each other. Sean drinks a lot, gets annoyed with Lauren and then tells her he'll pay for her abortion. Lauren has an abortion. Sean drives her back to campus, and she is angry at him. At a party Sean has sex with Judy, Susan and Katrina, and necks with the hippie girl.

### Commentary

Both Sean and Lauren are from wealthy families, and they both attend Camden, an exclusive college in New Hampshire. Sean has a motorcycle and a car, and he and Lauren take expensive drugs constantly. And yet somehow, when they visit the affluent married couple in New York, they are both repulsed by the couple's fancy possessions and plans to buy a foreign auto. We realize that despite their privileged backgrounds, comfortable living conditions and expensive material possessions, Sean and Lauren are actually bohemians at heart.

Ellis has said that *The Rules of Attraction* "is kind of the complete opposite of *Less Than Zero*—it might date back to the Beats and stream-of-consciousness writing." Like the protagonists of Beat novelist Jack Kerouac's *On the Road*, Sean and Lauren drive around aimlessly (in Sean and Lauren's case because they are trying to ignore Lauren's pregnancy). Despite all the mood-altering substances they ingest, the trip eventually sours and they are forced to face the problems at hand. Like other stream-of-consciousness writers, Ellis just keeps writing and writing the first thing that comes into his mind, because even though that's not how most people write, that's how many people think.

After Lauren has an abortion, there is a page in the book that is blank except for her name printed at the top. The author means to indicate that

Lauren's feelings of loss and emptiness are so profound and complex that describing them is beyond the scope of even his writing abilities. In a sense, this page is the most eloquent passage in the whole book. The bold authorial admission proves Ellis's willingness to make difficult personal sacrifices for his craft.

## XCVII–CV

### Summary

Mitchell and Sean go to buy some marijuana from Rupert. Rupert wants money from Sean, so he pulls out a big knife. A car chase ensues. Lauren goes to lunch with Franklin and takes a Xanax pill. By coincidence, their restaurant waiter is the "townie" to whom Lauren lost her virginity at the beginning of the book.

Sean packs his bags to leave campus. Sean tells Tim he really liked Lauren but that he didn't pay for her abortion, because he didn't like her that much. Victor runs into Lauren in the restaurant. He remembers having sex with her in the past but doesn't remember her name. He decides to go home with her anyway.

Lauren tells Paul that Sean likes him. Paul runs after Sean as he drives away, but finally he gives up and gets in a car with a man he barely knows. As he drives away, Sean picks up a "townie" girl. She starts telling him her life story, which isn't very interesting, but he squeezes her knee. The novel ends (as it began) in mid-sentence.

### Commentary

The very last section deals with the cyclical nature of life—and at the same time deals with the essentially random, disjointed nature of life in the late 1980s. Lauren's waiter at the restaurant is the "townie," now dressed, who helped deflower her in the first chapter. She is also finally reunited with Victor, who—though he doesn't recognize or remember her—decides to go home with her. At the very end, Sean gives a ride to a "townie" girl who starts telling him her life story. He remarks that it isn't very interesting, but he listens anyway. In a sense, the "townie" girl's story-within-the-story is a metaphor for the novel as a whole.

## QUESTIONS FOR REVIEW

1. *The Rules of Attraction* recounts approximately eight different parties from three different points of view. Would the novel be even better if it had one omniscient narrator and 24 parties?

2. Compare Sean's and Lauren's thoughts on the similarities and differences between cunnilingus and intimacy with those of Jay McInerney's heroine Alison in *Story of My Life*.

3. Read the following passage from *The Rules of Attraction* and then try to answer the questions:

   EVE: Mimi had two more vodka Collins and when the three of us left the dining room . . . she fell against the elevator attendent and almost passed out. I walked her back to her room where she took a Valiium and went to sleep. Paul went into the other room. I sat on the bed watching Eve sleep for quite some time before I decided to tell him.

   a) How can the character Eve watch "Eve" sleep?
   b) Doesn't Eve mean to say "Mimi"?
   c) What do you think of Ellis's statement, "An editor for me is someone who can correct my grammar more than anything else"?

4. Recounting his stay in Greece, Victor says, "My ass and dick got sunburned." In McInerney's *Story of My Life*, Alison showers with "some kind of weird black soap that stings my vagina, which is a little bit sore to begin with, granted." What is going on here?

## SUGGESTIONS FOR FURTHER READING

"Looking for Cool in L.A." (*Vanity Fair*, November 1985): "*Less Than Zero*'s Bret Easton Ellis chronicles his quest for the ultimate 'happening' place in L.A. with Brat Packer Judd Nelson . . ."

"Bad Bret" (*EYE*, September 1986): Mariarosa Sclauzero interviews Ellis.

Book review (*Los Angeles Times*, February 1, 1987): Bob Asahina, Ellis's editor at Simon & Schuster, reviews competing author David Foster Wallace's *The Broom of the System*.

"Page Six" item (*New York Post*, September 30, 1987): Cave Canem, a new restaurant in New York's East Village, throws a party for Ellis on its opening night.

"Page Six" item (*New York Post*, November 12, 1987): Ellis refuses to go to parties and premieres for *Less Than Zero* movie because he doesn't like the way it was adapted. Nonetheless, he tried to get thirty free *Less Than Zero* T-shirts at a *Less Than Zero* party at Limelight discothèque, but studio executives will only give him five.

"The Moveable Clubs that Cater to LA Nightlifers" (*Los Angeles Times*, November 27, 1987): Account of Ellis hosting party for author Mark Lindquist at Los Angeles nightclub but failing to show up because he's afraid to fly.

"Page Six" item (*New York Post*, December 2, 1987): Ellis hosts a party for author Mark Lindquist at the Tunnel discothèque in New York. At party, Ellis advises Lindquist to ignore critics.

"Page Six" item (*New York Post*, October 4, 1988): Ellis attends a party for *Town & Country* magazine's "most eligible women" at Le Club restaurant. Ellis says he is working on his third novel—*American Psycho*—about an investment banker who murders high-class prostitutes.

# *Story of My Life* by Jay McInerney

## LIST OF CHARACTERS

*Alison*
   The narrator. An aspiring young actress who lives in New York City. She takes acting classes, uses cocaine and has sex with many men.

*Dean*
   A well-heeled bond seller who used to be an actor and plans to retire early in order to write plays and novels. He and Alison become lovers.

*Skip*
   A commodities trader who was one of Alison's lovers. He used cocaine and gave Alison a sexually transmitted genital rash, but she got tired of him.

*Rebecca*
   Alison's sister, a self-destructive woman who uses lots of drugs, spends a lot of money and has sex with many men.

*Francesca*
   Alison's friend, who keeps computer files detailing her friends' sexual encounters.

## 1. "GETTING IN TOUCH WITH YOUR CHILD"

*Summary*
   Alison is mad at her wealthy father because he has not sent her money recently. Alison used to like horses, but when her horse died and she moved to New York, her interest turned to taking cocaine and having sex. She is also interested in acting classes.
   Alison calls Skip and fools him into thinking she's pregnant, so that he will give her $1,000 for an abortion. Alison talks to her sister Carol, and they agree that Skip is a "prick . . . just like Dad." Alison's roommate Jeannie comes home, and Alison gives her Valium, a prescription mood-suppressant pill, because she has taken too much cocaine.
   Alison goes to acting class and acts really crazy as an acting exercise, but the teacher makes her go home because she's acting too crazy. Alison's father calls. He is sad because his 22-year-old girlfriend has left him. Alison is mad at him, but she consoles him and persuades him to send the money.

*Commentary*
   In this first chapter, we are introduced to the Alison Poole character and some of the major themes of the novel. Alison's first-person narrative voice, full of slang and swear words, is a fairly accurate re-creation of a voice you

54

might hear from a member of certain New York social circles in the late 1980s. Also, McInerney uses no quotation marks when other characters say things; it's as if Alison herself is talking and talking, and thus telling us the "story of her life."

Alison says that people lie too often and that she believes in total honesty. She likes acting because it is "about being true to your feelings, which is great since real life seems to be about being a liar and a hypocrite." But is acting really honest? This conflict alerts us that as readers, we must "read between the lines," because Alison frequently says things that don't really make sense.

## 2. "SCENES FOR ONE MAN AND ONE WOMAN"

### Summary

Alison meets Dean Chasen at a discothèque nightclub named "Nell's" (which is an actual nightclub in New York City). Alison likes him and tells him she has slept with 35 different men. She wants to have sex with Dean also, but she still has a sexually transmitted genital rash that Skip gave her. They neck anyway. Alison gets so sexually aroused and frustrated that she curses Skip's name. Dean finds this off-putting, because he is a friend of Skip's and thinks that Skip is "a walking petri dish" of sexually transmitted diseases.

The next morning Alison calls Francesca, who berates Alison for not performing oral sex on Dean. Alison also talks to Jeannie, Didi and Rebecca, who have been taking cocaine all night.

Alison performs oral sex on Dean while he tries to eat his breakfast. Alison doesn't mind performing fellatio. She enjoys experiencing cunnilingus but finds it too intimate for a first date. She recalls an article in a fashion magazine that said an average dosage of human ejaculate is very high in calories. This article made her old boyfriend angry, since Alison was watching her weight at the time.

### Commentary

In this chapter, the author introduces some very graphic depictions of sex. This may shock us, but we must remember that he is only reporting shocking behavior that could actually happen in real life.

In a sense, Alison sees sex as a series of financial transactions: "I guess trading favors is what it's all about," she says. She "gives" Dean a "blowjob [a slang expression meaning an act of fellatio]." This makes her feel like an "angel or a nurse" doing a "good deed." In other words, sex can sometimes be like charity. The strongest example of this theory is her recollection of an old boyfriend who used to buy her one article of expensive clothing for each act of fellatio she performed on him.

Also, Alison sees sex as being more mechanical than emotional: she calls her left nipple "the button" and says she becomes very aroused when Dean, or anyone else, "pushes" it.

# 3. "SENSE-MEMORY"

**Summary**
Alison leaves Dean's apartment. The fellatio seems to have put him in a good mood. Alison thinks about her mother, who has begun to drink more and watch religious television since her divorce. Alison goes back to her apartment, where Didi and Rebecca are using cocaine. They want Alison to stay and take cocaine with them, but she leaves.

Alison goes to acting class. The class does an acting exercise about sharp tastes, so Alison pretends she's eating a hot Mexican pepper. Then she pretends that she's performing fellatio on Dean. The acting teacher finds her rendering so masterful that he tells everybody else to stop and watch. Afterward, they all talk about it.

**Commentary**
In this chapter, Alison takes a cab driven by a Russian émigré who is thankful for the luxuries available in America. This scene is an ironic commentary on social class differences in America. Alison has had many privileges in life, but she is not content. The Russian has had few privileges, but he is very content. McInerney uses this scene to bolster his thesis that privilege, wealth and social status make life more difficult for a person than poverty or underprivilege.

This chapter also contains two clues that Alison is an *unreliable narrator*. That she thinks the term "White Russian" means "Caucasian Russian" alerts us that Alison might not be very well educated.

# 4. "TRUTH OR DARE"

**Summary**
Dean comes over to take Alison out for an ethnic food dinner. Jeannie flirts with Dean because Alison once went out with Jeannie's fiancé, Frank. Later, Didi comes to Dean's apartment and they all take cocaine. Jeannie and Francesca arrive and they take more cocaine.

They play Truth or Dare, a game. Dean dares Didi to take off her clothes, which she does immediately. There is much sexual tension, due to the lighthearted discussion of sensitive topics. Then Alison's sister Rebecca telephones asking for money so that she won't get stabbed.

**Commentary**
The game of Truth or Dare is a frank commentary on the dangers of honesty. Even though Alison thinks honesty is the best thing, she does not like hearing Dean say he wouldn't mind having sex with her best friends. Alison herself doesn't "dare" to tell the truth when she rates Skip's sexual performance on a one-to-ten scale. Nor does she like it when Didi takes off all her clothes at Dean's request—even though Didi's nudity symbolizes complete honesty of a certain type.

56

# 5. "CARE OF THE SOCIAL FABRIC"

*Summary*
After Rebecca's call, they all go to a bad section of town and retrieve her from the apartment of a black drug dealer, Mannie, who said she owed him money.

Alison and Dean go to bed, take Valium pills and argue about the evening's events, particularly Dean's daring Didi to take her clothes off. Alison sleeps through acting class and then goes home to masturbate using the bathtub faucet. Because she is mad at Dean, Alison goes out with Brad, a man she hardly knows. They go to a stage play, and then Brad takes Alison home. He starts grabbing her, so she pokes him in the buttocks with a decorative brooch.

Jeannie has returned from a trip to North Carolina to visit her fiancé Frank. When she got there, she found Frank with another woman. She broke many of Frank's belongings and hit him with a champagne bottle and then came back.

*Commentary*
The concept of honesty is examined as Alison and Dean argue. She thinks that honesty is always best, while he thinks that "white lies" are often necessary. Alison seems to be a hypocrite: even though she says she values honesty, she frequently lies. But we must remember that she has had a hard life, despite (or, in fact, *because* of) her many material privileges, and that she is consequently not entirely responsible for her hypocritical behavior. In fact, the two things that *literally* hurt people in this chapter are an expensive brooch and a bottle of champagne—both symbols of wealth and privilege.

# 6. "TWO LIES"

*Summary*
At her acting class, Alison can't stop thinking about the enjoyable sexual relations she had with Dean the night before. Later, Jeannie tells Alison that they've received an eviction notice because Jeannie spent Alison's rent money on cocaine and fancy clothes.

Dean and Alison go to the nightclub "Nell's." While they're necking, Skip walks up. Dean leaves. Skip says that Dean recently went out with a woman named Cassie Hane. At home, Dean starts making sexual overtures toward Alison, but she is angry. Dean swears he did not have sex with Cassie Hane. Then Dean and Alison have sex, even though Alison is still angry.

*Commentary*
That this chapter is titled "Two Lies" is probably no accident. The title refers to a joke that Alison can only remember part of and keeps asking people to complete for her. The joke is that the three greatest lies in the world are: (1.) "The check's in the mail" and (2.) "I won't come [ejaculate] in your mouth." No one can remember the third lie, until the surprise climax of the

novel, when Everett tells Alison that the third lie is "I love you." This final, dark realization expresses the poignant hollowness of life in New York in the late 1980s.

# 7. "JUST CONTACT"

## Summary

The next morning Dean admits that he had sex with Cassie Hane. Alison leaves. Her phone service has been cut off because Francesca hasn't been paying the bill. Rebecca calls and says that she's in a hotel with a man who wants to marry her and that the black drug dealer, Mannie, wants to marry her also. Alison's old boyfriend Alex wants to come visit Alison and Jeannie. Alison knows he wants to have sex with Jeannie.

At Dean's apartment, Alison overhears Cassie Hane leave a sexually suggestive message on Dean's answering machine. Instead of getting angry, Alison demands that Dean have sex with her, which he does, twice. During the sexual act, Alison is interested only in her own satisfaction, but when it is over she notes that the experience wasn't satisfying.

## Commentary

Alison thinks it is unfair for wealthy parents to shower their children with money and gifts when they're young and then suddenly to expect the children to make a living on their own when they become adults. In a redundant but crucial explanatory passage, she says, "But it's, like, these goddamned fathers, they give us everything for a while and then suddenly they change the rules. Like, we grow up thinking we're princesses and suddenly they're amazed that we aren't happy to live like peasants."

McInerney wants us to understand that the reason Alison does not get a job and support herself is not that she is lazy or unqualified, but that her parents stunted her personal growth by never letting her learn to be independent.

Alison refuses to ask her grandfather for money to pay her telephone bill, because she thinks he is the only totally decent person she knows. This gives Alison yet another dimension: the only reason she does bad things to some people is that some people are not decent and do not deserve good treatment.

# 8. "SCENES FOR ONE MAN AND TWO WOMEN"

## Summary

At acting class, the teacher says that a healthy adult can tell the difference between fantasy and reality. Alison asks how this is done. The teacher suggests that Alison seek professional psychiatric help.

Alison calls Cliff, her father's right-hand man, who once tried to rape her in the family stable. At the time of the rape, her father didn't believe that the attack had happened and told Alison to be quiet about it.

Alison returns to her apartment in the morning. Alex and Jeannie have had sex. They all go out for a walk. They go to a sexual paraphernalia shop, and Alex buys electrical phallic devices for Jeannie and Alison. They go to the top of the Empire State Building, where Alison vomits.

*Commentary*

McInerney's writing about sexual habits (such as fellatio or the purchase of electrical phallic devices) and bodily functions (such as vomiting) is shockingly frank. The honesty with which he treats these subjects is much like Alison's honesty; the author and the main character are thus mirrored, and we see that McInerney's writing about Alison is a way of writing about himself. In a 1988 television segment, McInerney commented, "It was fun to be Alison Poole for the three or four months that it took to write this book. Sort of like slipping into a pair of these [holds up a pair of high-heel shoes]. . . . So maybe now people will stop assuming that I'm the hero of all my books. Maybe now they'll just assume I like dressing up in women's clothes."

# 9. "DERBY DAY"

*Summary*

Alison goes to a Kentucky Derby party that is attended by many men with whom she has had sex. They watch the famous horse race on television. Alison goes in the bathroom and feels nauseous. The horse she liked is taken out of the race because it has a nosebleed. Didi really wants some cocaine, but no one will give it to her, because she has quit using drugs. All the men pay attention to Rebecca because she's wearing a provocative dress and dancing around with a bottle of liquor.

*Commentary*

The nausea Alison repeatedly experiences is a popular literary metaphor. The French philosopher and novelist Jean-Paul Sartre introduced nausea as a form of *empathetic fallacy*: a person can feel physically ill due to being spiritually overwhelmed by the excesses of the modern age. Nausea is frequently used in the works of novelists such as McInerney, Ellis, Janowitz, Eisenstadt and McCloy to let the close reader know that a character is pregnant and will thus soon have an abortion.

The racehorse with a nosebleed is another twofold symbol. It foreshadows Alison's breakdown due to cocaine abuse, and it also foreshadows the revelation that Alison was psychologically scarred in her formative years when her father poisoned her favorite horse. The horse named "Capote" symbolizes the author's obsession with Truman Capote, a writer who was never able to match the success he had at a young age and who was, until he died, thought of more as a beau monde celebrity than as a writer.

# 10. "TRUTH OR DARE II"

*Summary*
    Later that night, they all go to Dean's apartment to drink liquor and take cocaine. They play Truth or Dare again. Skip rates Alison a nine (on a one-to-ten scale) as far as sexual performance but says that she never performed fellatio on him. Rebecca takes off all her clothes. Dean admits he has an erection. Rebecca grabs Dean's genitals.
    Alison goes to the bathroom and feels nauseous again. In front of everybody, Dean asks Alison if she's slept with Skip recently, and she admits that she has. Suddenly, Mannie, the black drug dealer who has a crush on Rebecca, runs in with a big knife. He is crying because Rebecca has forsaken him. While they try to take the big knife away from Mannie, he jumps out of a window.

*Commentary*
    The critic James Wolcott has theorized that Mannie's fall from the window is a metaphor for the scriptural fall of man ("Mannie" = MANnie). Alison and her friends always describe Mannie as a person who looks like Prince, a pop music entertainer. Thus it can be said that Mannie is a "Prince among men"—even though he is not from a privileged background and he "falls from grace" out of a sixth-floor window.
    Like Vladimir Nabokov and James Joyce before him, McInerney incorporates puns, wordplay and pop culture references into his story. The reader must be well versed in television, pop music and contemporary jokes to appreciate both levels of the novel. By employing these reference points, McInerney makes a daring statement—that mass culture (e.g., rock music, television shows) may be as valid as high culture (e.g., books). The familiar edict "Write about what you know" has not been lost on McInerney.
    Also, Mannie's demise points out another hidden danger of a privileged upbringing. Because of their sheltered lives, none of the characters has any idea how to restrain a black man with a big knife, so he jumps out of a window.

# 11. "HUNTERS AND JUMPERS"

*Summary*
    Alison wakes up feeling very nauseous. She finds out that both Dean and Skip have been seen with other women. Alison hasn't talked to Dean in two weeks. Didi has stopped taking drugs and has found religion. Mannie survived his fall. Nobody got in trouble with the police. Rebecca is in Switzerland with a new boyfriend. Jeannie and Frank have reconciled. Dean has started being more responsible about his work and personal life.
    Alison and Jeannie take some cocaine and then go to a nightclub. Alison has sex with Skip because she's mad at Dean. Alison has lunch with an unattractive but wealthy man who wants to buy the pearl necklace her grand-

60

mother gave her. She eats a lot and then vomits in the street. She gives the money to Jeannie, and they use part of it to buy cocaine. They stay up all night talking about friends and the old days when they rode horses together.

## Commentary

In this chapter—as in the final act of a seventeenth-century Restoration comedy—all the novel's loose ends are tied up and all the characters accounted for. But this is not the last chapter. McInerney, again employing Nabokovian techniques of multilayering, uses this *false ending* to render explicit the cruel fact that in real life, unlike in much fiction, things do not often have tidy or meaningful endings.

# 12. "GOOD NIGHT LADIES"

## Summary

Alison discovers that she is pregnant, but she's not sure which of the men she has had sex with is the father. She visits Mannie in the hospital. Mannie says he still loves Rebecca.

Alison has an abortion the day before her birthday and spends her birthday in bed. Then she gets up and takes a limousine to a restaurant with all of her friends. They take lots of cocaine. The party lasts for two days. Alison can't really remember what happened. She thinks she might have tried to jump out a window. She finally called the telephone number of a drug rehabilitation center Didi had given her.

Now Alison is in a rehabilitation center in Minnesota. She remembers her favorite horse—"Dangerous Dan." She loved that horse. Finally, she recalls, her father poisoned it and also sexually abused her. She calls her father and tells him that she thinks it might have been cheaper if he'd just killed the horse. He doesn't understand, and she suddenly wishes that all these things she remembers were only dreams.

## Commentary

Alison's visit with Mannie is rife with metaphorical significance. Even though Mannie's entire body is in bandages, he still loves Rebecca. In other words, Man can still love, even if he cannot feel or have sex. The other moral lesson is one of hope: Man *must* still love, even after he has been hurt— whether by sexual betrayal or by romantic indifference or by a leap from a sixth-floor apartment window.

The careful reader will note the irony of Alison having an abortion on the day before her *birth*day. Though the meaning of this dramatic juxtaposition is not clear, it is nonetheless important.

# QUESTIONS FOR REVIEW

1. Most people consider sex to be an act of intimacy, but Alison thinks just the opposite. What do you think? Alison also thinks that cunnilingus is not right on a first date. She says, ". . . sticking your face in someone's crotch—I mean, it's really intimate." What do you think?

2. McInerney suggests that the reason some women are nymphomaniacs is that they had bad experiences when they were younger. Do you agree?

3. A working familiarity with popular youth culture is vital to understanding this novel. Well-informed readers will note that the phrase "pearl necklace" is a slang euphemism for the act of fellatio. What, then, are the possible metaphorical implications when Alison sells her grandmother's pearl necklace to an unattractive but wealthy man?

4. When Alison tells her father that "it might have been cheaper if you just killed the horse," he doesn't understand. Do you? Please explain.

5. Although Alison's narration is very honest, it is often not very interesting. The same could be said of McInerney as author. What can boring fiction make us feel that interesting fiction cannot?

# SUGGESTIONS FOR FURTHER READING

"Page Six" item (*New York Post*, February 9, 1985): McInerney explains why he has never submitted fiction to *The New Yorker*: "I can't imagine my stuff in there. I don't have that muted, understated irony they like so much."

*Esquire* (April 1985): McInerney profiles pop musician Mick Jagger.

"Jock Strapped: Confessions of a Guy Who Couldn't Score" (*Mademoiselle*, June 1985): Personal essay about "how a nonjock learned to win with women."

"Page Six" item (*New York Post*, September 21, 1985): McInerney and Ellis spotted walking together in New York on way to party at Palladium.

"Dimmer Lights, Smaller City" (*The New Republic*, November 4, 1985): Review of *Ransom* by Ian Buruma.

"Couples for Whom the Initial Feeling Was Far from Mutual" (*New York Times*, February 2, 1986): McInerney's second wife, Merry, discusses how much she disliked him when they first met: "I thought he was slick and self-centered. . . . He was talking when I first came in, and he didn't let up all night. I thought he was very pleased with himself."

"Page Six" item (*New York Post*, February 26, 1986): McInerney's wife, Merry, is applying to graduate schools in Nashville and Bloomington, Indiana. McInerney says, "Any talk of leaving [New York] is premature."

"I'm Successful and You're Not" (*New York Times Book Review*, July 13, 1986): McInerney reviews Janowitz's *Slaves of New York*.

"Page Six" item (*New York Post*, May 25, 1987): McInerney throws a party for Ellis at a restaurant named Current. Tama Janowitz, Michael J. Fox and others attend.

"Page Six" item (*New York Post*, August 4, 1987): McInerney's companion, model Marla Hanson, contracts poison ivy during "a romantic country weekend" with McInerney.

"The Canal Bar" (*House and Garden*, April 1988): McInerney reviews a new New York City restaurant of which he is a habitué.

"How to Write and Get Anything Published with Jay McInerney" (Learning Annex catalog, November 1988): Advertisement for Learning Annex class McInerney taught.

"Yada Yada Yada" (*The New Republic*, October 10, 1988): Review of *Story of My Life* by James Wolcott.

"Page Six" item (*New York Post*, October 26, 1988): McInerney is seen at a party with Cornelia Guest, rather than his usual companion, Marla Hanson, or his wife, Merry.

"Page Six" item (*New York Post*, February 22, 1989): McInerney says rumors that his publisher, Atlantic Monthly Press, will be sold are prompted by "resentment of older publishers" who want to see the hip publishing house fail. McInerney explains that *Story of My Life* is Atlantic Monthly Press's bestselling book yet.

"Page Six" item (*New York Post*, February 29, 1989): McInerney's Hollywood agent, Jeremy Zimmer, has plans to make *Story of My Life* into a stage play, to premiere in London's West End and then come to New York.

# *American Dad* by Tama Janowitz

## BIOGRAPHICAL NOTE: See page 10.

## LIST OF CHARACTERS

### *Earl Przepasniak*
The narrator. His parents divorce and then his mother dies.

### *Bobo*
Earl's levelheaded brother.

### Dad
Earl and Bobo's self-centered father. He is a psychiatrist who smokes a lot of marijuana and dates young women.

### Mom
Earl and Bobo's delicate mother. She is a poet and a genius who likes to spend the day in bed and go to the library. She dies.

### Summary
Dad rules the family by intimidation. Earl has many pets, all of which die, go crazy or are sold. Mom and Dad divorce. Earl and Bobo move to a house on Mom's side of the property. The houses are connected by a bridge that eventually rots.

Dad remarries, to Maura, a psychiatric nurse, but doesn't invite the boys to the reception because all the guests are taking LSD. Two-and-a-half years later, Dad divorces Maura because she is sexually frigid. Dad loses his job, as the head of the mental health department at a women's college, for having sex with a patient. When Dad storms into Mom's house to have an argument over alimony, he accidentally upsets a postage meter, which falls on Mom's head and kills her. Earl testifies against Dad, who is put in jail.

Earl goes to Columbia University and falls in love with Maggie, a nymphomaniac who cheats on her boyfriend. She tolerates Earl, whom her parents hate, but they do not have sex. Maggie gets pregnant, has an abortion and becomes anorexic.

Earl wonders if he is homosexual. He goes to London. He meets Emma, and they have an affair until her boyfriend returns. Emma introduces Earl to Elmira. Earl and Elmira have sex. Elmira becomes pregnant. Earl demands she have an abortion. She declines.

Earl has an affair with a famous playwright and then returns to Elmira. Emma and Elmira are angry at him. They humiliate him by beating him in a Monopoly game and then forcing him to scrub the floor naked. In the course of these episodes, Earl comes to some realizations about masculinity and rites of passage.

Earl realizes that Dad always disliked him because he was the oldest son, and that Dad worried about being cuckolded by him. Dad has a chain-saw accident and maims himself. Earl returns home to care for Dad. Bobo goes off to college. Earl thinks about sending for Elmira and the baby.

### Commentary
Speaking of *American Dad*, Janowitz has said, "My father [a Freudian psychologist who divorced Janowitz's mother, a poet, and subsequently dated young women] is a bastard, but I've resolved that issue." Thus we see that besides the ability to entertain and inform, fiction can also be used to work out personal problems and achieve emotional catharsis regarding those who have hurt us.

# *Summer* by Lisa Grunwald

## BIOGRAPHICAL NOTE

Lisa Grunwald (b. 1959) attended Harvard College. She was 26 when this, her first novel, was published.

## LIST OF CHARACTERS

### Jen
The narrator, an 18-year-old college freshman and photographer. Her mother is dying of cancer.

### Lulu
Jen's mother, a vivacious woman who's dying of cancer.

### Daddy
Jen's father, a famous sculptor who has never done anything but sculptures of Lulu, his dying wife.

### Hillary
Jen's 23-year-old sister, who is a television-commercial actress.

### Ben
A fellow Jen has sex with during the summer.

### Summary
Daddy flies Lulu and Jen to the family's summer house on a small island off Cape Cod, which might be Martha's Vineyard. Lulu doesn't care to talk about her cancer. While photographing Daddy's studio, Jen decides that both her parents must die because they are deeply in love and she cannot imagine them apart. Jen cries because Daddy doesn't like the photos she took for a class. Hillary arrives and says that her current boyfriend Spencer isn't special and that "he's just a fuck."

Jen thinks her family is the most important thing in her life. Jen's published book of photographs arrives in the mail. Jen follows Daddy one morning and finds that he's building a makeshift studio in the woods. Daddy gets angry at her for following him. Spencer arrives. Jen overhears him having sex with Hillary.

Lulu falls and is confined to bed. Jen decides to take flying lessons from Ben so she can learn how to sabotage Daddy's plane and thus insure that Lulu and Daddy will die together. At a Fourth of July party, Lulu gets very sick but refuses to let her famous intellectual guests know. A drunk writer accuses Daddy of only doing the same sculpture over and over. Lulu tells him to shut up.

Jen finds Daddy in his studio assembling a carousel of horses rather than a sculpture of Lulu. Jen is jealous of Hillary's apparent ability to cope with Lulu's imminent death. Ben kisses Jen during her flying lesson. The doctor says Lulu's cancer has spread to her liver.

Ben and Jen have sex. Jen continues her plan to sabotage Daddy's airplane. Jen tells Ben that Lulu is dying. Then they have sex. Ben flies Lulu and Jen to Boston so Lulu can have medical tests. Lulu experiences bad pain on her birthday. Jen is now able to cope with Lulu's illness better than Daddy and Hillary.

Jen finds Daddy's almost-complete carousel and is angry that the sculpture isn't about Lulu, though it does contain images of the whole family and their friends. Jen goes to the airport and exposes her attempt to sabotage Daddy's plane, so that the accident will be averted. Jen uses an ax to knock down Daddy's studio so Lulu will see the carousel on her way to the airport. Lulu sees the sculpture and is happy. Ben flies Daddy and Lulu to Boston, where Lulu will die.

### Commentary

The famous Russian writer Leo Tolstoy once wrote, "All happy families are alike; every unhappy family is unhappy in its own way." Grunwald's autobiographical *Summer* succinctly updates this famous and important idea, as do most of the books of this genre: every unhappy family, in fact, is unhappy in the same way, because the mother is dead or dying.

# *Ransom* by Jay McInerney

## BIOGRAPHICAL NOTE: See page 1.

## LIST OF CHARACTERS

### Christopher Ransom
An American living in Japan, studying karate. His mother died of cancer when he was 14.

### Miles
An American friend of Ransom's who owns two bars in Japan.

### Devito
A former American marine who dislikes and eventually kills Ransom.

## Summary

Ransom avoids drugs and liquor due to an incident in his past. He hates his father, who makes second-rate television shows in America and was unfaithful to Ransom's mother before she died. Miles is attracted to Marilyn. Ransom reminisces about traveling with his friends Ian and Annette in Pakistan and the Far East. Ransom goes on a date with Marilyn. Ransom again remembers being in Pakistan with Ian and Annette. Ian was smuggling drugs across the border. Ransom's girlfriend Annette was a heroin addict. Ian got kidnapped, so Ransom injected Annette with heroin and sold her to a tribesman. Devito tells Miles that Marilyn and Ransom are having an affair. Marilyn tells Ransom that she was hired by his father to lure Ransom back to America. Ransom's father arrives in Tokyo and tries to persuade him to come home.

Devito challenges Ransom to a fight with swords. Ransom draws first blood but hesitates before going in for the kill. Then Devito cuts Ransom in two, killing him.

## Commentary

Examined in a historical context, *Ransom* makes more sense. Jay McInerney wrote most of the book—his first novel—while on a fellowship in Japan. The novel wasn't very good but after the enormous commercial success of *Bright Lights, Big City*, McInerney's then-publisher, Vintage Contemporaries, decided to release the book as McInerney's "second novel." Though *Ransom* met uniformly bad reviews and indifference in the marketplace, the story of an American living in Japan still symbolizes the clash of Eastern and Western sensibilities.

# *Highlights of the Off-Season* by Peter J. Smith

## BIOGRAPHICAL NOTE

Peter J. Smith (b. 1959) attended Columbia University. He was 27 when this, his first novel, was published.

## LIST OF CHARACTERS

### Sam Grace
A prep school student who has been kicked out of two different schools. His mother died when he was young.

### Bob Grace
Sam's father, who lives in New York City.

### Lucy Grace
Sam's sister, who lives in California and plays a rebellious nun on a network television show.

### Sarah
A girl Sam knew at his first prep school, in Massachusetts. He runs into her again when he visits Cape Cod.

### Ellis
Sam's dead mother's sister, who lives in Cape Cod, Massachusetts. Sam tries to visit her.

### Summary
Sam lives in Southern California with his sister. He has already been kicked out of a prep school in Massachusetts and now he is being kicked out of a California prep school. Sam's father has come to California to persuade him to return to New York and to consider going to prep school in England. Sam returns to New York and spends New Year's Eve with his two wealthy godfathers.

After Sam's father drops him off at the airport to go to London for school, Sam decides instead to go to Cape Cod and try to locate his Aunt Ellis. He stays in a motel and runs into Sarah. He also meets Ruth, a woman who works in the motel, and her fiancé. He finally calls his aunt and asks her if his mother left any message for him before she died, but his aunt says she didn't.

Sam takes a bus back to New York. He takes a nap in Central Park, and his shoes and wallet are stolen. He can't reach his father by telephone. He goes back to his father's apartment, but the new doorman doesn't recognize him and beats him up.

Sam wakes up in Sandstone, a mental hospital. He is sarcastic toward the psychiatrists, so they want to keep him for observation. A black patient named Anne knows he isn't crazy and encourages him to leave. He finally escapes and eventually gets back to his father's apartment. His father is mad when he finds Sam didn't go to London, but eventually Sam goes off to a new prep school.

### Commentary
Almost exactly like J. D. Salinger's *The Catcher in the Rye, Highlights of the Off-Season* follows a troubled teenager who gets kicked out of prep schools as he travels on his own through the Northeast, describing his misadventures in the cynical, humorous vernacular of a moody adolescent—with a denouement reminiscent of *One Flew Over the Cuckoo's Nest*, a popular novel among cynical, humorous, moody adolescents.

# A *Cannibal in Manhattan* by Tama Janowitz

**BIOGRAPHICAL NOTE: See page 10.**

## LIST OF CHARACTERS

*Mgungu Yabba Mgungu*
> The narrator. A cannibal who lives on the island of New Burnt Norton.

*Maria Fishburn:*
> A rich young heiress who takes Mgungu away from New Burnt Norton.

*Reynard Lopato:*
> A sinister, foppish criminal whom Mgungu falls in with.

*Mikhail:*
> A dwarf magazine writer who eats nothing but candy.

*Summary*
> Maria persuades Mgungu to fly to New York alone. On the plane Mgungu meets Kent Gable a bisexual Australian musician. At a party in New York, a stylish woman invites Mgungu to have sex, but she is sickened by his foot odor. Maria proposes marriage to Mgungu. Mgungu meets Joey, who runs a pizza parlor, and Mrs. Tuckermann, who runs a delicatessen. At a press conference, the reporters think Mgungu is a fake, because he is so articulate.
>
> Joey takes Mgungu to an oddly decorated nightclub. At a restaurant, Gable asks Mgungu to perform fellatio on him. Mgungu declines. Maria and Mgungu get married at a fancy restaurant.
>
> Mgungu goes to Maria's apartment, but Reynard tells Mgungu to go away because Maria is busy. The next day, Mgungu goes on a picnic with Reynard and Mikhail. Reynard has brought special meat for Mgungu. Mgungu eats it, but Reynard and Mikhail don't. Later, Mgungu discovers Reynard in Maria's apartment disemboweling an unidentifiable corpse. Reynard tells Mgungu that he should leave the country immediately to avoid being blamed for this crime.
>
> Penniless, Mgungu wanders around eating garbage off the ground and a squirrel. He begins drinking excessively. One day, Reynard arrives in a limousine and says that the meat Mgungu ate at the picnic was human flesh. Reynard's lawyer persuades Mgungu to sign some putatively helpful legal documents.
>
> Mgungu suffers delirium tremens. The newspapers say that Mgungu married Maria only to kill and eat her. He takes the stimulants amyl nitrate and cocaine and passes out. Later, policemen apprehend him.
>
> Mgungu is put in jail. He gets a large advance from Crown Publishers to write his memoirs, but he squanders all the money. Protestors picket the prison, supporting Mgungu's cause. Joey goes to Mgungu's island to live. Mgungu

talks to the prison psychiatrist and comes to some tentative conclusions about his life.

(The novel ends with a detailed two-page "Acknowledgements" spread in which the author thanks a long list of New York socialites, minor celebrities, clothing designers, hairstylists and photographers.)

### Commentary

The juxtaposition of a very sophisticated woman and a primitive man allows us to compare her civilized status and his savagery and ask "Who is really more civilized?"

Mgungu is an innocent, much like Voltaire's character Candide. He does not understand many things. He thinks that an airline meal is a "celebratory feast tray" and that Banana Republic is an actual country, rather than a retail clothing chain. The authorial intent of these repeated misunderstandings is humor and sometimes satire.

Even though Mgungu is not a skilled writer, he receives a lucrative contract from Crown Publishers—the very publisher of this novel. This is a final instance of Janowitz's wry use of the techniques of metafiction and autobiography.

# *Sad Movies* by Mark Lindquist

## BIOGRAPHICAL NOTE

Mark Lindquist (b. 1959) attended the University of Southern California. He was 28 when this, his first novel, was published.

## LIST OF CHARACTERS

### Zeke

A film school graduate who is writing ad copy for second-rate movies, rather than pursuing his goal to be a screenwriter. His mother is in an insane asylum.

### Becky

Zeke's girlfriend, an actress.

### Y. J. Ogvassed

An old friend of Zeke's who is mystically oriented.

### Summary

Zeke contemplates suicide on his 25th birthday. Throughout the book, Zeke drinks liquor, takes drugs and listens to the music of 37 different pop music combos. He goes to work at Big Gun Films, takes cocaine with his co-workers Wendy and Susie and then goes on a three-day "bender" with them. They go to a rock concert, have sex and take more drugs.

When Zeke tells Becky about this, she begins crying. Then they have sex. She encourages him to write more, so they'll have more money. Then she leaves him. Zeke contemplates suicide until Becky returns.

Y. J. Ogvassed comes to visit Zeke. Zeke tells Y.J. that he plans to commit suicide, and Y.J. says he will dissuade Zeke from doing this. Y.J. and Zeke go to a poetry reading, where Zeke reads a poem he co-wrote with Becky, entitled "Isn't It Fucked?" He receives a standing ovation.

Zeke and Becky engage in rough sex. Zeke, Becky and Y.J. drive to Big Sur, where Y.J. says some space aliens called Orgonians will appear and dissuade Zeke from committing suicide. They camp on the beach, and in the morning Zeke and Becky have sex. They return to Los Angeles, where Becky is a great success acting in the play *Waiting for Godot* by the existentialist Irish playwright Samuel Beckett. Then Zeke and Becky have sex. Y.J. tells Zeke he loves him.

Y.J.'s dog Blackie is being kept in the pound and is to be put to sleep. Zeke quits his job at Big Gun Films. Y.J. and Becky throw a party for Zeke. They free Blackie from the pound, and when they leave, Becky takes along a puppy she sees there.

Zeke stops taking cocaine. He tells Becky about his now-abandoned plan to kill himself. Then they have sex. For the time being, Zeke is confident that his and Becky's love is reason enough to go on living.

### Commentary

At one point, Zeke plays a drinking game called "Beerhunter," a version of Russian Roulette in which one beer out of a six-pack is shaken up to the exploding point. When Zeke realizes that he is stuck with the beer that will explode, he quits the game. This act symbolizes his rejection of suicide and his desire to go on living.

# *Outside Providence* by Peter Farrelly

## BIOGRAPHICAL NOTE

Peter Farrelly (b. 1956) went to Providence College and the Columbia University writing program. He was 32 when this, his first novel, was published.

# LIST OF CHARACTERS

## Tim

The narrator. His mother shot herself to death in 1963. He lives with his father in the working-class town of Pawtucket, Rhode Island.

## Tim's father

A gruff man who runs a radiator shop and calls Tim "Dildo."

## DeCenzo, Mousy, Drugs Delany and Tommy the Wire

Tim's working-class friends from Pawtucket.

## John Wheeler, Jack Rafferty, Irving Waltham, S.D. and Jane Weston

Tim's friends at Cornwall Academy.

## Summary

Tim and his working-class friends spend their time drinking liquor, smoking marijuana and causing mischief in Pawtucket. Tim's brother is paralyzed in an accident. Tim's father sends Tim to Cornwall Academy, an exclusive New England prep school. Tim's roommate, Irving Waltham, is a prissy, straitlaced type. Tim spends time with John Wheeler, a wealthy type.

Back in Pawtucket, Tim and his friends pledge to move to Arizona when they graduate. Tim dates S.D. and then breaks up with her. Tim starts liking Jane Weston. Back in Pawtucket, his father tells him gruffly to make something of himself. Mousy is killed in an automobile accident.

Tim learns that Jane likes him. Jane and Tim spend time in the woods together drinking liquor, smoking marijuana and talking. One day Tim learns that S.D. has been having sex with many fellows one after another over a period of a few hours. Tim tries to stop her, but she tells him that Wheeler made her pregnant and then stopped speaking to her after she had an abortion. Tim has sex with her and then takes her to the school nurse. S.D. commits suicide.

Tim, Rafferty, Irving and Jane go to Pawtucket. Tim and Jane almost have sex for the first time. Irving gets very drunk and becomes less prissy.

During their school break, Tim and Jane travel through the South and have sex a lot. Jane doesn't want Tim to use birth control. Later, Jane tells Tim she is pregnant and that she plans to have the baby. When Tim points out that Jane didn't want him to use birth control, she gets mad at him and leaves.

Tim and his friends are caught having a liquor and hashish party in their dorm room by Mr. Funderburk, a teacher. Irving takes the blame and is expelled, but he is proud because he is no longer a prissy, straitlaced type.

Jack confesses that he betrayed his friends by telling Funderburk about the party so that the school administrators would help him get into Brown University and become a lawyer. Jack also says he had sex with Jane before Tim did. Tim almost pushes Jack off the roof. The young, hip teacher Dave Swanson has a talk with Tim. Tim cries and finally admits he loves his father.

DeCenzo visits Tim at school and says he got his girlfriend Bunny pregnant. Tim swears off liquor and drugs for a while. He persuades DeCenzo to help Bunny have the baby. Tim says he will return to help his father.

Jane visits Tim in his room the night before graduation. Tim says he can understand how one can love a person and still let her go. Tim hitchhikes back to Pawtucket.

### Commentary

Like Eisenstadt's *From Rockaway*, *Outside Providence* examines the inner turmoil felt by a working-class adolescent from the Northeast thrust into the upper-class scholastic environment of an exclusive New England school. Like Ellis's *Less Than Zero*, the novel chronicles sexual convolutions and casual drug use among a small circle of young people at an exclusive New England school. Like McInerney's *Bright Lights, Big City*, it concludes with the protagonist realizing that he must change his life and stop indulging so many bad habits. Like almost every other novel in the genre, the aftereffects of a mother's death on a young man resonate throughout the story. Unlike the other novels, though, *Outside Providence* takes place at an exclusive New England *prep* school, like Salinger's *The Catcher in the Rye*.

# *Velocity* by Kristin McCloy

## BIOGRAPHICAL NOTE

Kristin McCloy (b. 1962) attended Duke University in North Carolina. She was 26 when this, her first novel, was published.

## LIST OF CHARACTERS

### Ellie Lowell
A 25-year-old theater student from North Carolina who lives in New York. Her mother is killed in a car accident.

### Tom Lowell
Ellie's father, a lonely, alcoholic small-town cop.

### Jesse
A long-haired, liquor-drinking half-Cherokee biker from Georgia, with whom Ellie has sex.

### Dec
Ellie's devoted boyfriend in New York. He is an aspiring documentary filmmaker and intellectual.

*Danny McKintyre*
Ellie's first love, who is now engaged to Ellie's high-school friend Melanie.

*Summary*
Ellie returns to her hometown to bury her mother. She takes a waitressing job at the local coffee shop. She meets Jesse and has sex with him. For the rest of the summer she works at the coffee shop, has sex with Jesse and avoids her father, her high-school friends and other important people in her life. Her boyfriend Dec comes to visit, and she avoids him also. She discovers that a friend of her father's had been having an affair with her mother before she died. Eventually Ellie discovers she is pregnant with Jesse's baby. She tells Jesse, but he wants no part of it. The next day, Ellie's father sends her back to New York.

*Commentary*
The story of an educated urbanite drawn to the dark, working-class side of life, and her subsequent pregnancy, captured by the author in an evocative rendering of malaise, places *Velocity* within the bounds of the genre. According to McCloy, the sex scenes were "the easiest parts to write . . . I would fall into a rhythm and it would get faster and faster, and I'd be typing my head off. And then it would be over, and I'd go, 'Rene [Echevarria, her boyfriend], wake up! Research!' "

# *Higher Education* by Lisa Pliscou

## BIOGRAPHICAL NOTE

Lisa Pliscou (b. 1960) attended Harvard College. She was 29 when this, her first novel, was published.

## LIST OF CHARACTERS

*Miranda Walker:*
A senior at Harvard who gets good grades without even trying, writes poetry, has sex with many men, uses cocaine, has a psychological eating disorder, hates her parents and is said to be witty. Her grandmother's death emotionally scarred her.

*Summary*
Miranda remembers having sex with Jackson on the couch in the college literary-magazine building. She remembers Bryan, with whom she used to have sex, being angry at her for having sex with a friend of his. Miranda remembers having sex with another fellow. Miranda thinks she is pregnant

74

because her period is overdue. She wants to have sex with still another fellow, Dean, whose girlfriend is Jennifer.

Miranda goes to the university medical clinic for a pregnancy test and finds out she is not pregnant. She meets Dean at a bar. Miranda's psychiatrist wants to know why Miranda hates her parents. Miranda remembers seeing Jackson kissing Wendy even though he had told Miranda he loved her.

Anson, a member of the college humor-magazine organization, encourages Miranda to join because she is so funny. She remembers talking to Henry, who couldn't understand why she broke up with him to date Jackson. Jackson and Miranda have sex. Miranda's mother calls, and Miranda pretends to be someone else so she won't have to talk to her.

Miranda and Richard take cocaine and have sex. She phones the university police to ask them to arrest the members of the college humor magazine for having an excessively noisy party in their building. Miranda goes to a "pajama party" at an all-male social club. She dances with Gerard, who gives her cocaine. Richard's pop music combo performs a song he wrote about Miranda.

At another party, Dean and Miranda dance. She sees Jackson kissing Stephanie. She discovers she is having her period. She remembers telling her father that she got accepted to Yale, Harvard, Princeton, Columbia and Stanford, with full scholarships to each. She remembers freshman year, when she felt that she didn't fit in socially and that the food was bad. She thinks about Henry, whom she misses.

In her writing class, Miranda is very critical of another student's story. She remembers her late grandmother, the only person she could really talk to.

Miranda visits Michael's room, but he doesn't want to have sex. She visits Jackson. She remembers how Jackson persuaded her to stop eating with the students who studied a lot and to instead eat with the students who dressed eccentrically. Jackson says that he had sex with her the previous Friday night only for fun.

Miranda cancels her psychiatric treatment. She remembers how her grandmother fell down some stairs and died, and how this emotionally scarred her. She gets accepted to graduate school at Columbia University. Richard says he has gotten a recording contract and is leaving for New York City. She tells Bryan that love means never having to say you're sorry.

Having finished her thesis, Miranda's roommate has finally discovered the meaning of life, which is: If you have one pimple, be grateful that it is only one. If you have two, be grateful that it is only two, and so on. Miranda decides to take things "one step at a time, as Gram might say."

### Commentary

As a workmanlike imitation of Ellis's *The Rules of Attraction, Higher Education* is a success. It has all the ingredients of a standard novel of the genre: the setting is an exclusive New England college; the protagonist feels like an "outsider"; the characters have a great deal of sex, take a variety of drugs and are virtually indistinguishable from one another; and the dialogue accurately evokes the hollow, awkward conversation of characters in undergraduate stories. Pliscou tests the bounds of the genre by hinging the plot on the traumatic death of the protagonist's *grandmother*, rather than her mother.

Close readers will also note the complex psychological subtext: the autobiographical heroine, Miranda, believes that she is remarkably witty and funny, but nothing she says in the book is witty or funny. In this sense, the novel's major themes are self-delusion and unrealized aspiration.

## *Other Novels of the Genre*

A few other novels are sometimes mistakenly included in the genre. David Foster Wallace's *The Broom of the System*, for instance, follows the adventures of Lenore Stonecipher Beadsman in the Cleveland of the 1990s. Though Wallace was 24 when this, his first novel, was published, the book's supposedly Pynchonesque complexity marks it as an ineffectual oddity—the "Jabberwocky" of the genre, so to speak.

Nancy Lemann's *Lives of the Saints* is (according to the jacket copy) the story of "a southern belle misplaced in an eastern college for the past four years [who] has returned to contemporary New Orleans." Despite Lemann's efforts to carve out her own niche in what agent Amanda "Binky" Urban affectionately calls the *And-Then-They-Fucked* genre, Lemann's novel fails to deliver in a Janowitzian sense.

Mary-Ann T. Smith's *The Book of Phoebe* tells of a pregnant Yale senior who goes to Paris to have her baby. In Paris, she comes to terms with a deep, dark secret from her childhood. Smith's effort to place herself in the genre is highly calculated and well conceived. Unfortunately, at 41, she is too old.

The death of a mother does not automatically place a novel in this tightly defined genre. In her novel *Monkeys*, Susan Minot has committed a crucial error by designing a plot in which the mother's death is not a critical plot point and justification for her children's misbehavior later in their lives. In fact, the novel (which is actually a collection of short stories) traces a family's life over the years *before* the mother dies. Minot's over-reliance on acute, evocative prose and often crisp dialogue is a weakness that excludes her work from the genre.

Michael Chabon's *The Mysteries of Pittsburgh* is also frequently included in this genre, primarily because of Chabon's relative youth, the large publishing advance he received and the fact that the protagonist's mother is dead. In fact, the book does not fit in the genre at all. Chabon's characters are not glamorous-but-unhappy urbanites, and the novel's strong, compelling plot appeals to the vulgar interests of readers who prefer diversion and entertainment rather than being confronted with the hollow malaise of life in the 1980s chronicled in the many novels which *do* define the genre.

## SUGGESTED THEME TOPICS

1. Just as McInerney's *Ransom* and *Story of My Life* sold more poorly than *Bright Lights, Big City*, and just as Ellis's *The Rules of Attraction*

sold fewer copies than did *Less Than Zero*, *A Cannibal in Manhattan* did not do nearly as well as Janowitz's first novel, *Slaves of New York*. Discuss this in light of Janowitz's theme of the fleeting nature of celebrity.

2. Ellis has said that people miss the humor in his books, and in fact, Ellis's books do include many jokes. Of these punchlines from *Less Than Zero* and *The Rules of Attraction*, which do you think is funniest?

   a) "Spaghetti moves when you eat it."
   b) "The rat, oblivious to the elephant's wounds, said, 'Suffer baby, suffer,' and kept on fucking."
   c) "Because the last time I fucked a nigger she stole my wallet."

3. Contrast any one of the books in the genre with a well-written twentieth-century novel of your own choice.

4. In Ellis's *Less Than Zero*, Clay sees a vanity license plate that reads "GABSTOY." Discuss Ellis's self-styled similarities to F. Scott Fitzgerald and the difficulty of creating a humorous yet accurate anagram of the surname "Gatsby."

5. Which of the following observations by Alison in *Story of My Life* is the most eloquent and moving?

   a) "Story of my life." (page 2)
   b) "Story of Skip's life, trading commodities." (page 3)
   c) "Story of my life." (page 8)
   d) "Story of his life." (page 15)
   e) "Story of my life." (page 18)
   f) "He wants to tell me the story of his life. . . ." (page 37)
   g) "Story of my life, right?" (page 58)
   h) "Story of Rebecca's life." (page 116)
   i) " . . . story of my life, talking to machines . . ." (page 124)
   j) "Story of my life." (page 133)
   k) "Story of his life." (page 153)
   l) "Story of her life." (page 167)
   m) "Story of his life." (page 178)

6. Eleven of the 15 books in the genre use the *dead mother* plot device. Is this because

   a) in the 1980s most young people's mothers died before the young people turned 25?
   b) most of the authors are still at the age when they hate their parents?
   c) each author was convinced that his or her own adolescence was much more traumatic than everyone else's, and a fictional dead

mother is a convenient gambit to justify misbehavior and whi-
niness?

7. Try to think about Tama Janowitz for a while.

8. Choose the best punchline for this joke, which features prominently
in McInerney's *Story of My Life*: "The world's three biggest lies are
'The check's in the mail,' 'I won't come in your mouth' and . . .

   a) 'I love you.' (Everett in *Story of My Life*)
   b) 'I'll pay you back' (Alana in *Less Than Zero*)
   c) 'Jay, those critics are just jealous!' (James Wolcott in *The New Republic*)

9. Editor Morgan Entrekin once said, "Gary [Fisketjon] and I are kind
of known as the 'disco publishers.' " Try to imagine a social milieu
in which this sobriquet would be considered something other than a
source of future ridicule.

10. One thing almost all of these authors have in common is that they
attended university "writing workshops." What can a writing class
teach a future novelist that getting a real job and developing his or
her craft over a period of years cannot teach?

11. Who's cooler—McInerney or Ellis? Prove it.

12. Try to tell the difference between at least five characters in *The Rules
of Attraction* or *Higher Education*.

13. Compare the characters of Injun Joe, Becky Thatcher and Muff Potter.

14. One purpose of bleak, lackluster writing about adolescent angst is to
make the reader appreciate the rich wonder of real life. Can you think
of a passage from any of these novels that was so bad that it made
you smile or even laugh?

# MASTER GENRE-IN-A-NUTSHELL COMPARISON CHART

| Book | Author's Age at Time of Publication | Reported Publisher's Advance | *Estimated Sales |
|------|------|------|------|
| *Bright Lights, Big City* | 29 | $7,500 trade paperback | 367,000 trade paperback; 253,000 mass-market movie tie-in |
| *Slaves of New York* | 29 | $7,000 hardcover; $85,000 trade paperback | 25,000 hardcover; 175,000 trade paperback; 150,000 mass-market movie tie-in |
| *Less Than Zero* | 21 | $5,000 hardcover; $99,000 paperback | 75,000 hardcover; 180,000 trade paperback; 150,000 mass-market movie tie-in |
| *From Rockaway* | 24 | $20,000 hardcover; $30,000 trade paperback | 8,000 hardcover; 19,000 trade paperback |
| *The Rules of Attraction* | 23 | $150,000 hardcover; $150,000 trade paperback | 20,000 hardcover; 40,000 trade paperback |
| *Story of My Life* | 33 | $200,000 hardcover; $350,000 trade paperback | 20,000 hardcover (according to the *New York Post*) or 85,000 (according to the author) |

*The sales figures for the mass-market movie tie-in versions do not reflect unsold copies eventually returned to the publishers.

| Movie Rights Optioned or Sold? | Sex Acts Depicted | Explicit Depictions of Drug Use |
|---|---|---|
| Yes | heterosexual (1), lesbian (1) | cocaine (12), Valium |
| Yes | heterosexual (6), lesbian (1) | heroin, marijuana |
| Yes | heterosexual (10), homosexual (4), ménage à trois (2) | cocaine (16), marijuana (9), Valium (4), heroin (3), Quaaludes (3), animal tranquilizers, Celestone, Decadron, Desoxyn, freebase cocaine, Lithium, LSD, Nembutal, Novocain, Thorazine |
| Yes | heterosexual (1) | marijuana |
| Yes | heterosexual (35), homosexual (13), masturbatory (4), ménage à trois (2) | marijuana (16), cocaine (5), Ecstasy (4), hashish (3), LSD (3), crystal methedrine (2), Xanax (2), Actifed, amphetamines, cough syrup with codeine, heroin, mushrooms, Ritalin, Seconal |
| Yes | heterosexual (11), masturbatory (1) | cocaine (11), Valium (3) |

*cont'd*

# MASTER GENRE-IN-A-NUTSHELL COMPARISON CHART
*cont'd*

| Book | First Line |
|---|---|
| *Bright Lights, Big City* | "You are not the kind of guy who would be at a place like this at this time of the morning." |
| *Slaves of New York* | "After I became a prostitute, I had to deal with penises of every imaginable shape and size." |
| *Less Than Zero* | "People are afraid to merge on freeways in Los Angeles." |
| *From Rockaway* | "The limo driver, Russ or Gus, has a bald, tan head and a line of whitish crust on his lip edges." |
| *The Rules of Attraction* | "and it's a story that might bore you but you don't have to listen, she told me, because she always knew it was going to be like that, and it was, she thinks, her first year, or, actually really a Friday, in September, at Camden, and this was three or four years ago, and she got so drunk that she ended up in bed, lost her virginity (late, she was eighteen) in Lorna Slavin's room, because she was a Freshman and had a roommate and Lorna was, she remembers, a Senior or Junior and usually sometimes at her boyfriend's place off-campus, to who she thought was a Sophomore Ceramics major but who was actually either some guy from N.Y.U., a film student, and up in New Hampshire just for The Dressed To Get Screwed party, or a townie." |
| *Story of My Life* | "I'm like, I don't believe this shit." |

**Last Line**

"You will have to learn everything all over again."

"He found himself smothered in her tremendous breasts, and he could hear her muffled laughter as she ripped the tape and started to wrap it around his wrists."

"Images so violent and malicious that they seemed to be my only point of reference for a long time afterwards. After I left."

"The guy on the left is my good friend Chowderhead and the other one, holding up the big fluke, that's me."

"She started telling me her life story, which wasn't very interesting, and when Rockpile came on singing 'Heart' I had to turn it up, drowning out her voice, but still I turned to her, my eyes interested, a serious smile, nodding, my hand squeezing her knee, and she"

"I'd love to think that ninety percent of it was just dreaming."

# MASTER GENRE-IN-A-NUTSHELL COMPARISON CHART
*cont'd*

| Book | Epigraph | Mentor |
|------|----------|--------|
| *Bright Lights, Big City* | excerpt from *The Sun Also Rises* by Ernest Hemingway | Raymond Carver |
| *Slaves of New York* | excerpt of Dorothy's dialogue from the movie *The Wizard of Oz* | Andy Warhol |
| *Less Than Zero* | lyric excerpts from songs by pop combos X and Led Zeppelin | Joe McGinniss |
| *From Rockaway* | none | Joe McGinniss |
| *The Rules of Attraction* | excerpt from Tim O'Brien's Vietnam novel *Going After Cacciato* | Jay McInerney |
| *Story of My Life* | excerpt from introduction to *The Oresteian Trilogy* by Philip Velacott | Gary Fisketjon |

| Agent | Editor | Gimmick |
|---|---|---|
| Amanda "Binky" Urban | Gary Fisketjon | Second-person narrative voice |
| Amanda "Binky" Urban | William Shawn/ David Groff | Book marketed as a roman à clef about celebrities, but bookbuyers were not informed that the "celebrities" were not really very well known |
| Amanda "Binky" Urban | Bob Asahina | Book marketed more as a thinly veiled documentary than as a work of fiction |
| Morton Janklow | Terry Adams | Written by a very young author who attended the same college at the same time as Bret Easton Ellis |
| Amanda "Binky" Urban | Bob Asahina | Fourteen different narrators; un-edited stream-of-consciousness writing; from the author of *Less Than Zero* |
| Amanda "Binky" Urban | Gary Fisketjon | Female narrative voice; from the author of *Bright Lights, Big City* |

84

# *The Authors Speak*

A *SPY NOTES* Simulated Roundtable Rap Session with authors Jay McInerney, Bret Easton Ellis, Tama Janowitz, Jill Eisenstadt, Peter Farrelly, Nancy Lemann, Lisa Pliscou and Kristin McCloy
(Featuring a special contribution from editor Gary Fisketjon)

The following comments were collected from magazine, newspaper and television interviews with the authors. They have been edited together to simulate the kind of no-holds-barred intellectual free-for-all that might occur if one could gather seven young urban novelists in a room and promised to publish what they said.

*First of all, most of you—*

MCINERNEY: "I won't talk about restaurants or girls."

*Okay. Tell us a little about your most recent books.*

MCINERNEY: "[At the nightclub Nell's] I was asked to sit down by a friend, and when he took off, I was left listening to the conversation of his sister and some of her friends. The language they were talking amazed me . . . the way they talked about men and sex. . . . I tried to reproduce it in prose."

ELLIS: "I don't know how people are going to handle [*The Rules of Attraction*]. I think it's really weird. . . . [It] will have the same concerns as the first one: keeping tabs on my generation."

*But how do you explain the uniformly negative reviews?*

ELLIS: "Once you have a first book that is that popular and that big, then really no matter what the literary merit of this [second] book, you will be the excuse to attack it."

MCINERNEY: "People are polite to first novels. Now we have the rudeness factor. It would be crippling to take this to heart."

ELLIS: "Jay [McInerney] will call me and say, 'Did you read what they wrote about us today?' and he'll be so upset he'll lose a day's work. I try to tell him it doesn't matter, but he takes a lot of it personally."

GARY FISKETJON: "It's all sour grapes. Jay could have written the St. James Bible and people would have panned it."

JANOWITZ: "My feelings are hurt, and you feel like 'oh how could you say this,' but it doesn't bother me that much because what can you do, you're writing the best book you can. And the other side of me feels glad they trashed it because mostly the books that I don't like are the ones getting the lovely reviews."

*You all basically write about yourselves, right?*

ELLIS: "The bad thing with a first novel is everyone thinks it's autobiographical even if it's not. With *Less Than Zero* everyone assumed that I was a coke-snorting, zombied, bisexual child molester just because the narrator was. . . . That person was not me. That person who was narrating that book who was not me was passive to a zombie-like degree."

MCINERNEY: "Nobody could survive much more than a week of this kind of [*Bright Lights* life], let alone write books . . . I'm too young to be a one-note kind of guy when I have a more symphonic mind."

FARRELLY: "[No.] It's just that I have to write about what I know. . . . The family thing is totally different. I have a great family."

EISENSTADT: "The people who don't know me are going to think it's auto-biographical. . . . I write about an Irish community and I'm not Irish."

PLISCOU: "*Higher Education* is first and foremost a work of fiction. There are many aspects of my heroine's character and personality that have nothing to do with me—her remarkable sangfroid, for one."

MCINERNEY (on *Story of My Life*): "[reads excerpt from book] Clearly, this isn't me talking. . . . It was fun to be Alison Poole for the three or four months that it took to write this book. Sort of like slipping into a pair of these [holds up a pair of high-heel shoes]. . . . So maybe now people will stop assuming that I'm the hero of all my books. Maybe now they'll just assume I like dressing up in women's clothes."

*You're all notorious for spending a lot of time in nightclubs and discothèques. What's the attraction?*

EISENSTADT: "I don't really like clubs. . . . Whenever I go to a club, which is rarely, it's too crowded to dance, it's too loud to talk, it's too dark to really observe anything, so I just end up sort of standing around. . . . I've never been to Nell's—that's the truth."

ELLIS: "I don't really like clubs either. . . . The scene in L.A. was pretty dead; in New York it seems even deader."

MCINERNEY: "I'm actually starting to not go places where I know I'll get spotted. I'm tired of it all."

JANOWITZ: "Believe me, if I went out as much as they said I did, those books wouldn't be lying around today."

LEMANN: "You can't just chronicle other writers hanging around in night-clubs."

*Bret, Jill, Lisa . . . of all the books in this genre, yours are by far the least funny. That's no easy feat. Please explain.*

ELLIS: "A lot of my writing is misunderstood. I think a lot of it is really funny."

EISENSTADT: "If you're overtly funny, then it's not funny."

PLISCOU: "Although I can trade repartee with the best of them, I must say I admire [my protagonist's] wry and infallible quick-wittedness."

EISENSTADT: "Also, you never really know if people have the same sense of humor as you do."

*Who are your influences?*

ELLIS: "Hemingway was the first writer as media celebrity, a supposedly glamorous thing. . . ."

MCINERNEY: "I think the most important writers for me are the Modernists like Hemingway and Joyce. They're quite different but they're two writers that I admire very much, also Fitzgerald, particularly *The Great Gatsby*."

ELLIS: "[*The Rules of Attraction*] . . . might date back to the Beats and stream-of-consciousness writing."

*You must be happy to have so much success and so many opportunities at such a young age. Right?*

ELLIS: "Everyone likes to think writers make so much money. I thought I had to, but if you're a young unmarried male in the highest tax bracket, whatever you make, 50% is gone, so whatever you have is split in half and then you have an agent who takes 10% and if you have another Hollywood agent, which I do, that's another 5 or 10%. . . . People should not think I'm wallowing in roomfuls of cash."

JANOWITZ: "The truth is, [people who say mean things] are just jealous of me. Now, why that should be I don't know. I'm just as miserable as the next person."

*Most of you are more well known as celebrities than as writers. Do you enjoy this?*

JANOWITZ: "I was never like a movie star, someone trained to get all the attention. I still don't feel like a celebrity. I still don't know what they're talking about."

MCINERNEY: "In *Ransom*, the young protagonist dies toward the end of the book. I thought that might make people think twice before saying, 'Is it you?' But instead they say things like, 'Why'd you kill yourself in the end?' Of course I say, 'Because dead authors tend to be more famous than living authors.' "

JANOWITZ: "It's so awful to be promoting yourself."

ELLIS: "I believe in, more or less, humbleness."

MCINERNEY: "Look at *me*. Look at Harold *Brodkey*. Look at Robert *Stone*. Look at *me*. Look at *Mailer*. Completely different models. Don't tell us what we should fucking do. Why shouldn't fiction be all over the map? I think somebody ought to be doing what I'm doing. So I'm doing it.''

*What do you think of each others' writing?*

**ELLIS:** "[McInerney's *Story of My Life*] is a very good book. It has a very consistent voice and is both very dark and very funny. It's a slight book—I mean it's not great literature in that sense. But I think it's exciting and I liked it.''

**MCINERNEY:** "On a scale of cool to hot, [Ellis and I are] at opposite ends, and there's more light at the end of my tunnel.''

**ELLIS:** "This [unpublished story by Eisenstadt] is the silliest garbage I've ever seen.''

**ELLIS:** "The characters [in Eisenstadt's *From Rockaway*] are really sweet and nice. I hope people don't think it's just an East Coast version of *Less Than Zero*, which it absolutely isn't.''

**JANOWITZ:** "McInerney did his thing—I do mine. I don't know why people compare. His characters live in New York and go to clubs, so do mine. That's all.''

**PLISCOU:** "*Bright Lights, Big City*, the most celebrated of those 'Brat Pack' works, went down like candy to me. It was light and easy and very glossy. That's not all bad, and my book does share some of that kind of gloss. But I think *Higher Education* has a seriousness about it and a depth of feeling that I never found in those other books. For one thing, my heroine, Miranda Walker, is an outsider.''

**ELLIS:** "Tama is the first Warhol writer. Her attitude about the literary establishment is very Warhol. People feel that that aesthetic shouldn't intrude on the so-called serious literary world.''

**MCINERNEY:** "I feel that Alison [Poole in McInerney's *Story of My Life*] and her friends are, in their way, as interesting as John Cheever's suburban couples and Raymond Carver's lumberjacks.''

*What exactly is your book about?*

**ELLIS:** "When interviewers ask, 'Well, what was *Less Than Zero* about?' I'm always tongue-tied.''

**EISENSTADT:** "You never really know what to tell people what happens in the book or what it's about. Those are really two different things. You don't want to tell people what it's about.''

**ELLIS:** "I guess I'm writing about—it always sounds so grandiose—about chronicling this generation.''

*Bret, you keep mentioning "chronicling your generation." What exactly are you talking about?*

**ELLIS:** "Though I know that every year we all like to think that the incoming [Bennington College] classes and younger students aren't as wise as we were, and that they aren't as bright as we were, and that they aren't as knowing as we were (even though we might not have been), I don't think there's any question about the last couple of incoming classes of this new generation: We *were* more knowing. We *were* brighter. We *were* wiser."

*Much of your writing seems most successful as personal therapy of some sort . . .*

**EISENSTADT:** "Even when you write badly, you're still getting something out of yourself."

**MCCLOY:** "[The sex scenes were] the easiest parts to write. . . . I would fall into a rhythm and it would get faster and faster, and I'd be typing my head off. And then it would be over, and I'd go, 'Rene [Echevarria, her boyfriend], wake up! Research!' "

**ELLIS:** "My book is a gesture of aggressiveness. It was an important thing for me to write."

*Bret, parts of your books are so poorly written and ill-conceived that they contain actual mistakes. Why?*

**ELLIS:** "An editor for me is someone who can correct my grammar more than anything else. I don't like to look upon it as a collaborative effort."

*Tama, you've been uncharacteristically quiet. What makes you mad?*

**JANOWITZ:** "I hear that people say [I] only got there because of Andy Warhol or because [I'm] pretty."

*That seems hard to believe.*

**JANOWITZ:** "Either I'm too isolated off writing, or I'm talking all the time. I'm getting a little bored with myself."

*That's a little more plausible. Anything else?*

**JANOWITZ:** "Yeah, I like to dress up in crazy dresses. . . ."

*And you too, Jay . . .?*

**MCINERNEY:** "In my third novel . . . I wanted to really put myself in someone else's shoes—go where no man had gone before, so to speak. So I eventually decided to put myself in a pair of high-heel pumps. Size six-and-a-half or so."

*Any sanctimonious thoughts about drug abuse? Anyone?*

**MCINERNEY:** "At one time I thought it was the height of human aspiration to know where the good club was, to be able to get into it, and to have enough drugs to be able to stay up."

**ELLIS:** "I did go through a period where I was doing a few drugs, yeah. . . . I also did a lot of drugs when I went to Bennington, Vermont. There seems to be this whole drug culture and it's spreading. It's not a good thing."

**MCINERNEY:** "People are waiting for me to pull a Fitzgerald in my life and die of an overdose."

*Bret, your second novel was even drearier than your first. So there's nowhere to go but up, right? Or . . .*

**ELLIS:** "I play keyboards. I write songs and music. . . . I'm getting something together in New York in the fall. I'll give it a shot for a year."

**MCINERNEY:** "By the time I'm sixty, I'm probably going to do what Norman Mailer has done recently: direct."

*Final thoughts?*

**ELLIS:** "Morality definitely is your own code of ethics day by day expressing individualism. I believe in individuality. If I have a moral code of ethics that I think people should have, individuality would top it off."

**MCINERNEY:** "As long as I'm keeping my mental and physical health intact and am continuing to write, if I really sustain a high level of dialogue with my past work and the work of those writers I admire, my work is not going to be limited in appeal to those who are interested in the chronicle of a certain era. It will also have rewards for people who are interested in American fiction—and maybe even world fiction."

*What?*

# BECOMING THE LITERARY VOICE OF A GENERATION
*How the Experts Do It: A Surefire 20-Step, 10-Year Plan*

Have a painful adolescence, as all adolescents do. Believe that your adolescence was much more painful than any other in history.

Go to exclusive northeastern college. Develop reputation as best fiction writer on campus. (It's easier than you think.)

Submit fiction to college literary magazine. Write stories almost unreadably far ahead of their time in unorthodox use of grammar, punctuation, organization.

Take writing class taught by middle-aged writer whose out-of-print first novel was said to have shown promise by *The New York Times* and who has been taking notes for "the big one" for 15 years.

In class, be brutally honest criticizing classmates' stories because you have duty to serve cruel, implicit truths—that life is empty and painful, that narrative organization is essentially deceitful and that you're a better writer than they are. Mock in particular those classmates who believe in beginnings, endings, character development and rewriting. Share marijuana with teacher.

Submit stories to *Esquire, The Atlantic, The New Yorker, Quarterly*. Receive form rejection letters at off-campus mailbox you've rented so that no one will know you're getting rejection slips and so that if you do sell a story, it will look effortless.